Available Titles from Frontier 2000 Media

Non Fiction:

No Regrets: How Homeschooling Earned me a Master's Degree at Age Sixteen

Writing for Today

Looking Backward: My Twenty-Five Years as a Homeschooling Mother

Adult Fiction:

The Fourth Kingdom

The Twelfth Juror

Children's Fiction:

Tales of Pig Isle

Foreword

The first week in September of 1975 I began teaching my oldest daughter Alexandra using a curriculum that I had devised myself. I had developed a phonics-based reading program, and most of my efforts were focused on teaching her to read. In addition, I used flash cards to teach her the one hundred basic addition and subtraction combinations. My curriculum also included teaching her to print, to write the numbers from one to one hundred, and to tell time.

To most people these would seem like simple enough accomplishments, but I was not most people. I was a clueless young mother who had no idea of how I should go about teaching anyone anything. I had only a high school education myself, and, to make matters worse, I knew no one to whom I could turn for advice.

Homeschooling was almost unheard of in those days. In fact, the term "homeschooling" had not yet been coined. I had met a Mennonite missionary family who homeschooled while the family traveled, but as soon as they arrived at their various destinations, the children were enrolled in the local schools.

In the strictest sense, the Mennonite family could not really be considered homeschoolers. They were, however, the only people whom I had met who had done any schooling outside the system. As a result, Susan, the mother, played an important role in giving me the courage to make a commitment to homeschooling. When they were in El Paso, she and her husband attended the same Saturday night prayer group that my husband John and I did. Although I had seen Susan only two or three times previously and had never had a conversation with her, one Saturday night I confided to her that I was considering homeschooling but was afraid that I would not be able to do it.

Susan replied, "You can do it, Girl. I only went to the eighth grade, and I can do it. It's not hard."

I do not recall ever seeing Susan again, but I replayed her remarks in my head a thousand times. I was, however, still far from convinced. It took a lot of prodding from my husband and a lot of prayer on my part before I was ready to take that giant step. It is probably a blessing that I had no idea that it would be eight years before I would meet another homeschooler.

With everyone I knew, except John, telling me that homeschooling my children was probably the worst idea that I had ever concocted, I began teaching Alexandra one month before her fifth birthday. I was terrified! I can still recall the cold fear I felt that warm sunny afternoon when I sat down with her at our kitchen table and began a twenty-five year odyssey that would take us to places that we had not yet even dreamed of going.

On that first day, however, I was concerned only with the present. What if I could not teach Alexandra to read? If I could not teach her to read, I would not be able to teach her anything else. Our homeschool would be history. I would have failed my husband, my child, and myself. No Olympic athlete, crouched with his toes on the starting line to begin his race for the gold medal, has ever felt more pressure than I did on that first day of school.

It came as a pleasant surprise, therefore, when teaching Alexandra to read proved to be fairly easy. Within six weeks she was reading simple children's books. I had chosen Dr. Seuss books as her primers, and they were so interesting to her that she really enjoyed learning to read them. In a few short weeks she mastered printing the alphabet and writing the numbers from one to one hundred. I also taught her the basic one hundred addition and one hundred subtraction combinations. With the help of a little red plastic teaching clock that I bought at a school supply store, I taught her to tell time. In six weeks I had succeeded in teaching my child those basic skills that I believed were necessary to justify my becoming her home teacher.

When Alexandra was five years and four months old, John and I enrolled her in the home study course through Calvert School in Baltimore, Maryland. She and I, thus, began a formal course of homeschooling that would take her from the first through the eighth grade, high school, undergraduate work and graduate studies.

We embarked on a twelve-month school year, five days a week, approximately three hours a day. The result was that Alexandra earned her Master of Arts in the Humanities from California State University at the age of sixteen. However, that eleven-year journey was strewn with obstacles that would nearly derail us on numerous occasions.

Because homeschooling was so new, simply locating schools that provided home study courses to complete all degree requirements was an enormous challenge. A great deal of prayer, combined with practical searching that involved asking the right people the right questions, was necessary to locate quality, accredited institutions.

For grades one through eight, our attorney helped us locate Calvert School. At the time we enrolled Alexandra in Calvert School, it was used by U. S. Foreign Service employees who were assigned to overseas locations where schools were either non-existent or unsatisfactory. It was also used by more than one-hundred missionary boards for their missionaries who were working in remote areas where schools were not available. Although Calvert School is secular in nature, because it was used by so many Christians, it was very respectful of Christian values and never included material that Christian parents would find offensive.

By the time she was ten, Alexandra was finishing the eighth grade, and we began looking for a high school that would allow her to continue her home study. The Headmaster at Calvert School recommended the American School in Chicago, Illinois. Because we knew that we were going to need to be able to verify that the children had actually completed each grade level in order for them to be able to progress to the next level, we had taken the Advisory Teacher Service through Calvert School. This allowed us to send all of the children's tests to the school where they were graded. Grade transcripts were recorded for each student so that they would be available when they were ready for high school. Even though she was only ten years old, Alexandra had a paper trail that verified that she had completed grades one through eight with outstanding results.

After reviewing Alexandra's grade transcripts, which were sent to the American School directly from Calvert School, the principal allowed us to enroll her at the American School. We choose the college preparatory course of study. I took the lead in selecting her electives, concentrating on additional literature and history courses. To my amazement, Alexandra sped through the high school curriculum at such a rate that, even though I "slowed her down" by reducing her school day to about two hours, she completed the four year course in eighteen months.

It soon became apparent that we needed to begin searching for a university that would allow Alexandra to earn her bachelor's degree at home. We contacted both the principal of the American School and the headmaster of Calvert School, but neither of them knew of such an institution. However, one of them recommended that we order a copy of *Peterson's Guides: Who Offers Part Time Degree Programs* which listed colleges and universities offering distance learning. We ordered the guide, but when it arrived, I was dismayed to discover that it consisted of several hundred pages of listings of colleges and universities in alphabetical order. The problem was that most of them offered very limited courses, and almost none allowed a student to actually earn a degree through home study.

The internet as we know it did not exist. The only way to explore the possibilities was to contact each individual college or university via "snail mail" and hope that eventually they would respond. I realized that this would never work. I felt overwhelmed and discouraged, so I put the book away and tried to clear my head.

I spent the next three days in prayer and then sat down with *Peterson's Guides* on my lap. After one final prayer, I closed my eyes and allowed it to fall open. To my horror, when I opened my eyes, I was staring at the listing for Brigham Young University. I knew, of course, that, academically, BYU was an excellent university, but it was also a Mormon university. As a fundamental, evangelical Christian, I knew that there was no way that God was going to have us involved with a Mormon university. I quickly fanned the pages over my thumb to smooth out any kinks that might have been responsible for this error and closed my eyes again. I then prayed and allowed *Peterson's Guides* to fall open for the second time. When I opened my eyes, I was, once again, staring at the listing for Brigham Young University.

I was certain that there was something wrong with the book that caused it to automatically fall open to that particular place so I called the older children to come into the family room. I then asked each of them to allow *Peterson's Guides* to fall open while they sat with their eyes closed. For each of them it fell open to a different listing, but it never fell open to the listing for Brigham Young University.

By this time I was really frustrated. I waited for John to come home and asked him to let *Peterson's Guides* fall open for him. He accommodated me, and the book fell open to a different listing. I grabbed the book and sat down again. After a quick prayer, I allowed it to fall open for the third time. It fell open to Brigham Young University.

We decided that we would check out BYU, and, as usual, John initiated the telephone contact. After he had talked to the various heads of the Degrees by Independent Study Program, they asked him to have Alexandra make a cassette tape talking about her educational experiences to date and detailing her plans for the future. After listening to the tape, the program director contacted Calvert and the American Schools and had her grade transcripts sent to them. Within a couple of weeks she had been admitted to the Degrees by Independent Study Program at BYU.

I had been skeptical about enrolling her in a program through a Mormon university, but the experience turned out to be everything that John and I had hoped it would be. All of the course materials were devoid of anything that might be objectionable in terms of sexual content, language, or the advocating of any alternative lifestyle. Although the degree program did include as a graduation requirement a course on the teachings of the Mormon Church, because she was studying at home, we were able to discuss these teachings in contrast with Biblical teachings. As a result, her faith was not shaken, and she now understands more about the Mormon Church than most Mormons who have never lived in the Salt Lake Valley.

Alexandra entered BYU in the fall of 1982 and completed all of her course work in two and one-half years. However, she still had to attend her closure seminar where she would make an oral presentation of her thesis. The thesis had been completed and accepted by the university, so it was only a formality, but the oral presentation was a necessary component for graduation. For that reason, she did not officially graduate until August of 1986.

In the meantime, we wanted to get her started in a graduate degree program. We narrowed it down to two, and discovered that Brigham Young University was actually working in concert with California State University at Dominguez Hills—one of our choices—to help them create an undergraduate degree program through home study. Cal State already had a liberal arts graduate degree that seemed to be the perfect next step, and Jim Rawson, the director of the program at BYU recommended this program highly. We would, however, have to convince Cal State to allow Alexandra to begin earning credits before she officially graduated from BYU.

Jim Rawson helped us accomplish this goal by writing a letter of recommendation to Dr. Lewis at Cal State assuring him that Alexandra's work was of "exceptional senior level quality" and that "she is eligible for graduate work."

I made the initial inquiries, and Alexandra sent an application and a letter to Dr. Lewis, the director of the program at Cal State. A week later we decided that it might be a good idea for her to phone Dr. Lewis directly to find out the status of her application. When he answered the phone, Dr. Lewis told Alexandra that Jim Rawson was sitting in his office and that they had been discussing her when the call came through. She was enrolled in the Master's Degree program immediately. Eighteen months later, at the age of 16, Alexandra graduated from Cal State with a GPA of 3.84.

All of the children were enrolled in the same programs and progressed through them at the same rate. Since the schools had been located, and we knew the procedures involved in having the children accepted into each school, much of the stress was eliminated in enrolling subsequent children.

Looking back, I realize that God was with us every step of the way. When my two youngest boys graduated from BYU, Dr. Ralph Rowley, who was then the director of the Degrees by Independent Study Program, announced that this was the final graduating class. BYU was closing the program! He then mentioned that the program had begun in 1975—the same year that I first sat down at my kitchen table and began teaching Alexandra with a program that I had devised myself.

Do I still think my copy of *Peterson's Guides* had some sort of defect that forced it to fall open to BYU? Years later, after my last child had graduated from BYU, I sat down with *Peterson's Guides* on my lap and closed my eyes. I still wanted confirmation that I had made the right decision, and I allowed it to fall open. When I opened my eyes, I was staring at the listing for BYU.

Perhaps, through the BYU experience God was teaching me something about trusting Him. I certainly have learned that His ways are not our ways. I have also learned that life is full of surprises and obstacles that seem insurmountable. If we are to have any hope of finishing the work He has for us, we must learn to put our lives in His hands.

Fortunately, when I began teaching Alexandra, I had no idea how complicated life would become. On my first day as a homeschooling mother I naively believed that teaching would be the most difficult part of homeschooling. I soon discovered, however, that actually teaching my children was easy compared to the other challenges I would face.

As each of the other nine children approached their fifth birthdays, I began working with them in my program, and when they were five years and four months old, we enrolled them in the Calvert School program. Each of the children followed the same schedule and was enrolled in the same programs. My foray into homeschooling was an academic success.

Perhaps, rather than worrying about how I was going to teach my children at home, I should have concentrated on how I was going to keep the home running while teaching my children. When I began teaching Alexandra, I was pregnant with my fifth child. Ultimately, I would give birth to ten children in less than thirteen years. That meant that I would be giving birth and adding a new student nearly every year for quite a while.

I had always been well organized, but I soon discovered that I would need to get *Super* organized if I were going to be able to deal with the various responsibilities of my new position of wife/mother/home teacher.

My non-teaching responsibilities fell into four major categories:

1. Family—Caring for my preschoolers and spending time outside of school with all of my children.
2. Housework—Cleaning, cooking, etc.
3. My homework—Preparing myself for the following day's lessons.
4. Spiritual training—Bible reading and family prayer.

As I began to explore all of the implications of a long-term commitment to homeschooling, I constantly tried to find ways to make more efficient use of my time so that I could devote the proper attention to each of these four areas. In doing this I made a wonderful discovery: *The better organized I was, the easier it became to accomplish that goal.*

In 1989 Alexandra published *No Regrets: How Homeschooling Earned me a Master's Degree at Age Sixteen,* a personal narrative about her experiences as a homeschooled child. *No Regrets* gives a much more detailed account of the schools the children attended and the various courses that they took to earn their degrees. It also gives in-depth information about many aspects of our homeschool that I have not included in this book.

To our surprise, soon after *No Regrets* was published, she and I began receiving invitations to speak at homeschool events around the country, and we became major speakers at homeschool conventions in various states. In addition, I testified before two state legislatures and was called as a witness in *Leeper vs. Arlington,* the landmark case that legalized homeschooling in Texas.

Whenever we spoke at the homeschool conventions, the other speakers had people manning their booths while they made only occasional appearances of between five and ten minutes to sign books. Afterwards, they disappeared so that they could "rest" until time for them to speak again.

Alexandra and I never did that. We believed that if someone goes to the trouble to locate you, invite you to speak, and pay your expenses and an honorarium to hear what you have to say, they deserve your undivided attention. Whenever we were not speaking, we were at our booth talking to people and answering questions.

Although we had a few minutes at the end of each session for Q & A, I realized early on that women will frequently not ask the question they most want answered because they don't want to reveal anything too personal to hundreds, or sometimes thousands, of strangers. If, however, they can ask that same question one-on-one, they will do it in a heartbeat. Therefore, every time I closed out a session, I said, "I will be at our booth all day between speaking sessions. If any of you would like to come by to talk, I would love to meet you." The result was that between my speaking sessions I stood on my feet in high-heeled shoes talking non-stop to other homeschooling mothers. At the end of a twelve-hour day, I was dead tired, my voice was hoarse, and my feet felt as if they needed to be amputated. Yet, those were some of the most rewarding days I have ever spent.

I just loved those women; I knew exactly how they felt. As I talked to women in New Mexico, Texas, North Dakota, Kansas, Oklahoma, Montana, and New York, I discovered that we all had one thing in common: *One of the greatest obstacles we faced was dealing with all of the extra-curricular demands on our time.* The most frequently asked questions were not about how to teach a particular subject but how to deal with preschoolers, and laundry, and meals.

As a result of those conversations, I prepared sessions that dealt with time management, discipline, and various topics that most frequently came up in these one-on-one conversations with homeschooling mothers.

Twenty years have now passed since Alexandra and I began speaking to homeschool groups. However, I was recently advised that there is still a need for the conversation. Today I cannot invite you to come by my booth to talk, but I would love to continue that conversation.

I have taken my original notes out of mothballs and expanded them with insights that time restraints kept me from including in my sessions at our speaking engagements. Nothing in my original sessions was based on theory; every comment and piece of advice was a direct result of what I, personally, had experienced as a homeschooling mother.

I have taken this same approach in preparing this narrative for homeschooling mothers. All of the techniques discussed in this book are ones that I utilized throughout my twenty-five years as a homeschooling mother, and I know they work. This is not a collection of ideas that sound good in theory but will not work in practice. These methods worked for me, and they will work for you.

I am certain that if I had not learned the various approaches discussed in this book I would never have been able to complete the monumental task of homeschooling my ten children. Ultimately, it is the little things that cause homeschooling mothers to give up and say, "I just can't do this." This book is about conquering the little things. I hope that whether you have one child or twelve, my story will bless you and help you overcome some of the challenges that only a homeschooling mother faces.

LOOKING BACKWARD

My Twenty-Five Years as a Homeschooling Mother

Joyce Swann

Frontier 2000 Media Group, Inc.

Cover Design: Stefan Swann
Copyright © 2010 by Joyce Swann
Published in the USA by Frontier 2000 Media Group Inc., El Paso, Texas.

ISBN-13: 978-1456505905
ISBN-10: 1456505904

DEDICATION

This book is dedicated to all of those homeschooling parents who are out there every day fighting the good fight. I hope it will encourage you to fight on.

This book is also dedicated to my ten children who served as a test case for homeschooling. Thank you to:

Alexandra

Christopher

Francesca

Dominic

Victoria

Benjamin

Israel

Gabrielle

Stefan

Judah

This Call Is for You

Setting Up Your School Hours

When I began homeschooling, people frequently asked me how I found time to work in the church. I was often asked about how I found time for my "ministry." When I explained that I did not have time to work in the church and take care of my family too, I met with some pretty strong criticism. I soon discovered that most people believed that spending all of my time teaching and caring for my husband and children was a big waste of time. How could I be really concerned about my responsibilities as a Christian and never "do anything" for Christ?

For a long time, I was embarrassed when the subject came up. I lamely defended my position by saying that I just did not have time to do more than attend church. In addition to Sunday services, I gave the children a good deal of spiritual instruction at home. We had daily Bible reading and daily family prayer. As they grew older, we added scripture memorization to this list. However, I could not volunteer for committees and all sorts of other church-related activities and still take care of my rapidly expanding family.

After several years of unsuccessful, red-faced stuttering and stammering when asked to defend my position, I came across the perfect answer to that question. The answer may or may not have satisfied my critics, but it satisfied me completely. From that day forward, I no longer felt embarrassed or defensive when asked about my apparent lack of Christian service.

One day one of my little students' vocabulary lesson contained the word "vocation." The Calvert manual said that the word "vocation" comes from the Latin *vocare* which means, "calling." As I read that simple definition, for the first time, I realized the significance of my homeschool.

Teaching my children at home was not an experiment; it was not a job, it was not even a career. Homeschooling my children was my vocation—my calling. It was real missionary work. When I began to understand that my homeschool was my ministry, my perspective changed. Although I had always taken my homeschooling responsibilities seriously, the work had suddenly taken on a much deeper spiritual quality. I was working for Christ, and He deserved my very best.

Clearly Define School Hours

I had always observed clearly established classroom hours, but when I understood the magnitude of the work I had accepted, I was more conscious than ever of the importance of adhering to those hours. If you are going to have a successful homeschool, you must understand that without clearly defined school hours, your homeschool will fall short. Therefore, it is imperative that you set up regular school hours. Homeschooling mothers are often tempted to fit their school hours into their schedules. As a result, just getting through each day is a challenge.

I can assure you that every single day you will be able to find ample reasons to not have school that day or to cut your assignments short. If you wait for a convenient time during the day to call your school into session or take a laid-back approach that allows various students to set their own hours and complete their assignments in their bedrooms or lying on the couch in the family room, your homeschool will suffer. Never adopt the attitude that you will make the schedule fit your life; you must make your life fit the schedule.

As a homeschooling mother, you must set up a schedule that works for you and your family and then adhere to it. From time to time, it will probably be necessary to adjust the schedule to accommodate the changing needs of your students. Certainly, a high school senior will not have the same needs as a first grader. However, both need to have regular school hours and reasonable expectations concerning the amount and quality of work they will perform each day.

Our homeschool had some constants that continued for our twenty-five year involvement. We also made adjustments as we added more students and the older children entered more advanced school work.

Establish a Start Time for Your Homeschool

When we began homeschooling, Alexandra was not quite five years old, and I was pregnant with my fifth child. Consequently, I found it very difficult to schedule my day so that I would have time for my homeschool. We began our school every morning at eight-thirty and ended our morning session at nine-thirty. Every afternoon at one o'clock I put the younger children down for their naps, and Alexandra and I resumed our lessons. This schedule allowed us to have an afternoon session during which we would not be interrupted by the younger children.

Although with the passing years other changes were made to our school hours, for the entire twenty-five years that our homeschool was in session, we always began our school day at eight-thirty. This gave us a starting point that never varied. Whatever else had to be changed, everyone knew that school began each day precisely at eight-thirty.

Adjust Your Schedule to Meet Your Needs

As I added more children to my classroom, it was no longer practical to have most of the school hours in the afternoon. I then changed our school hours to reflect our current needs. Our new school hours were eight-thirty until eleven-thirty. At eleven-thirty we broke for lunch and then resumed school from one until two o'clock.

Normally, no child's school day exceeded three hours, but these new hours gave me the flexibility to allow a child who needed some individual instruction to leave the classroom early during the three morning hours and then come back to school in the afternoon when I could work with him alone. This proved very effective in meeting the specific needs of each child and ensuring that each had the benefit of personal instruction.

Frequently, we did not need to go back to school at one o'clock, but that time was set aside for school. On the days when everyone was finished by eleven-thirty, I felt that I was taking an afternoon holiday. The psychological benefit of feeling that I had been rewarded by a "short" school day rather than feeling that I had been penalized by a "long" one was enormous. I might need to go back to school only one or two afternoons each week, and that meant that I had three or four "mini holidays" on the other afternoons.

I did have a few tricks that helped ensure a short school day—both for my children and me.

Texting—Th Hmsch Moms Bf

I began texting in 1975 and used it very effectively in my homeschool. In fact, I would have to say that texting was a major contributor to our success and soon became my new best friend. No, it was not the kind of texting that kids do using their big thumbs on teeny-tiny keyboards that send weirdly-coded messages to itty-bitty screens.

Our kind of texting involved textbooks. Because we used accredited courses for all grade levels and enrolled each child separately, every child had his own brand new set of textbooks. Since these books were not going to be handed down to subsequent students, I had an opportunity to utilize all texts as if they were consumables.

Those of us who attended public schools were thoroughly indoctrinated to believe that marking in a textbook was akin to committing a crime. Of course, the thinking was that if these books were defaced they would not be suitable for use by subsequent students. However, when you homeschool and are going to purchase new books for each student, that "logic" is no longer logical. My rule is this: *The books are made to serve you; you are not made to serve the books.*

A student can spend hours copying sentences to underline the subject once and the verb twice. Why? When you own the books, all you have to do is instruct your student to underline the subject once and the verb twice right in the book.

An exercise that would have taken half an hour can be completed in five minutes. The best part is that all of the benefits of the grammar lesson still apply. Absolutely nothing is lost to the student by not spending time copying material.

Likewise, when my students learned their spelling words for their weekly tests, I quizzed them orally and had them spell the words aloud. Since each student had a different spelling list, nothing could be accomplished by having them write the words. I kept track of any words they missed and had them restudy to be quizzed on those missed words the following day.

When students were instructed to compile a list of words and their definitions from their lessons in geography, science, etc., I told them to highlight those words and their definitions in their textbooks and to study from the texts rather than writing them on a separate sheet of paper.

Math books can also be used as consumables. Addition, subtraction, and multiplication problems can frequently be worked directly in the book. Of course, as math becomes more advanced, that is no longer possible, but whenever it makes sense, have your students work directly in their texts.

It's Simple—Not Easy

History records that Christopher Columbus was sitting at dinner with a group of Sea Captains who were belittling his discovery of the New World. They all agreed that the discovery amounted to "nothing" and that any of them could have done the same. Discovering the New World was "easy."

After a while Columbus held up a hard-boiled egg in its shell and asked who among them could make it stand on end. Each of the captains tried with no success. Columbus remained silent as the men became more and more frustrated until one finally announced, "No one can make an egg stand on end. It is impossible!"

Columbus then took the egg and set it down on its end just hard enough to slightly flatten the bottom. When he removed his hand, the egg stood on end perfectly. "Look!" he exclaimed. "It is easy, now that I have shown you how."

Clearly, standing an egg on end is not easy. In fact, it is not even possible unless you know how. Columbus had taken an impossible task and made it simple, not easy.

You should always look for ways to make homeschooling simple; you will, however, never be able to make it easy. During my twenty-five year tenure, I constantly looked for ways to make homeschooling simple for all of us.

The problem with simple is that few people respect what is truly simple. As I became better known in the homeschooling community, I was contacted by numerous homeschooling parents who wanted information about my methods. When I shared those methods with them, however, they were frequently disappointed.

For instance, I developed a phonics program to teach a child to read before I ever sat down with Alexandra and began our daily lessons. I mentioned earlier that I believed that if I could not teach my children to read I would not be able to teach them other things so I put quite a lot of thought into my little program.

I took 3 x 5 cards and wrote one letter of the alphabet on each. I then wrote common combinations such as *sh, ch, tr,* etc. on other cards. I taught Alexandra the name of each consonant and the sound it makes. I then taught her the name of each vowel and the long and short sound for each. After that I taught her the various common combinations. When she had mastered all of the cards, I introduced Dr. Seuss' *Hop on Pop* as her first reader because it utilized many of the combinations she had learned. Within six weeks after I first sat down with her she was reading.

People asked me if I were going to sell my "reading course" so that others could use it too. I explained that it was not something that anyone would buy because it was not a "reading course"; it was just a simple method of teaching someone to read.

Finally, I agreed to share the complete program with a friend who insisted that she was desperate for a way to teach her child to read. I copied every card for her on a new 3 x 5 card and invited her to come over to pick them up. When she arrived, I sat with her and explained exactly how I used the cards to achieve the desired results. (By this time I had taught five or six of my children to read using this method, and each of them had achieved the same results, so I knew positively that it worked.) My friend listened quietly and then took the cards and left.

Later, I walked out into the front yard and found the entire stack of cards scattered over the lawn. She had thrown them away, and had not even done me the courtesy of waiting until she left my property to do so! I felt the full impact of the slap in the face that she had just given me.

This woman had a lot of money and spent it freely. If I had produced a program that included colorful artwork, glossy cards and complex instructions, she would have gladly paid me three or four hundred dollars to get it. Whether it would have actually worked would not have been an issue. She would have had something showy and something that her other friends might envy.

The other thing my friend wanted was a method that was easy. Everyone wants something that they can just give to their children that will enable them to teach themselves. NO SUCH METHOD EXISTS. IF YOU SEE ONE FOR SALE, PUT YOUR HAND OVER YOUR WALLET AND RUN IN THE OPPOSITE DIRECTION.

My method was incredibly simple, but it was not easy. During those six weeks I sat with my students every day practicing with those cards. I heaped on the praise as they mastered each one, but I often felt like jumping out of my chair and screaming. It was tedious; it was boring; it was time consuming; it was effective.

When my children were in Calvert School and were solving math problems using the metric system, one of their Calvert teachers commented when she returned a test that this was the only time she had ever had a student get the metric problems right. She wanted to know how we were teaching metrics.

What I was doing was simple. In the USA metrics, for all practical purposes, do not exist. A child will never learn them through any sort of daily use, and, as far as he is concerned, they will never translate into anything real. I, therefore, taught metrics by teaching my students to move the decimal point to the right or left, depending on the measurement involved. I had them memorize a little chart that I devised so that whenever they were working problems involving metrics they could draw the chart and fill it in themselves. Each time they encountered metrics I required them to reconstruct the chart—no saving the chart for the next use. They then used their chart as a guide to move the decimals. The result was that both in their daily work and on their tests they scored 100% perfect on all problems involving metrics.

Simple? Yes. *Easy?* No. I spent a considerable amount of time teaching each of my students the basics of solving the metric problems. I told them that no matter what the problem instructed them to do, I did not want them to consider whether they were dividing or multiplying; if they would move the decimal point according to the chart, they would always have the right answer.

When the children were required to memorize stanzas from *The Twins* by Henry S. Leigh, I realized that because of the poem's rhythm, it could be sung to the tune of *Supercalifragilisticexpialidocious*. By learning the poem as a song, they were able to master their recitations quickly. The assignment became simple.

Every subject I ever taught became a target for simplification. Ironically, when something becomes simple it also becomes memorable. I am astonished at how much the children have retained from those early lessons now that they are adults. Thoreau wrote, "Our lives are frittered away by detail. Simplify, simplify." I would paraphrase him: *Don't allow your homeschool to be frittered away by detail. Simplify, simplify.*

Busy Work Is Never Done

Before she began homeschooling, my daughter Victoria enrolled her daughter Fascia in a Christian school for the first and second grades. One day I asked Fascia what she liked best in school and, after a moment's thought, she replied, "Bible study."

I then asked her what she really disliked, and without any hesitation she replied, "Seat work."

My daughter Alexandra was present when we were having this conversation, and she looked puzzled. Later she asked me what Fascia was talking about. I explained that "seat work" is just another name for busy work. Alexandra was genuinely surprised to learn that children in traditional classroom settings spend a large part of each day performing tasks expressly designed to keep them occupied until the clock strikes three-thirty and they can go home and begin their homework!

Avoid the pitfalls of "busy work." Always be on the lookout for ways to eliminate things that are merely time fillers—time wasters actually—and look for ways to help your children use every minute spent in the classroom actually accomplishing something.

When Is The "Wrong" Answer The "Right" Answer?

When I was in the first grade, the class was given a test that included the question, "Can monkeys talk?" I answered, "Yes."

Later, when we children were working at our desks while the teacher graded our tests, I heard Miss Walski scream, "Joyce Degele! How could you have missed this question! You're the only one in the class who got it wrong!"

Miss Walski then proceeded to ask me—at full volume and in front of the entire class—whether I really believed that monkeys could talk. I answered that I did. She became even more agitated, and her face grew redder as she bellowed that I couldn't possibly believe that monkeys can talk to people.

I replied that I did not believe that monkeys can talk to people, but I did believe that they can talk to each other. She then informed me in tones loud enough to wake the dead that the question asked whether I think monkeys can talk to people.

I remained quiet, but I was thinking, *"That's not what the question said. It said, 'Can moneys talk?' They must be able to talk to each other because they make noises all the time that all of the other monkeys understand."*

I was only six years old, and since I normally scored 100 percent on my tests, I was especially embarrassed to be singled out to be ridiculed in front of the entire class for not knowing the "right" answer. However uncomfortable that experience may have been, Miss Walski did not succeed in convincing me that monkeys cannot talk. I have never deviated from my original premise that monkeys can and do "talk" to each other.

This was a good life lesson for me because it made me aware that the "right" answer is not always the correct answer. When I taught my children, I always listened carefully to their answers, and no matter how outrageous they might seem on the surface, if the child could give me a good reason for coming to a particular conclusion, I would agree with him that the answer had merit and might even be the more correct answer, but I then explained why the textbook answer was the one the school wanted.

The following are some examples of situations from my homeschool that really made me think:

Example 1: When Christopher was six years old and in the third grade, the Calvert course introduced science. One of the first lessons showed pictures of a tiger, a tree, and a rock. The student was asked to identify which was an animal, which was a plant, and which was a mineral.

Christopher did this part of the assignment without difficulty, but then the book asked the student to identify the group to which people belong. Christopher immediately responded that people do not belong to any of those groups. I was surprised that he could miss something so obvious so I tried to steer him down a path that would help him come to the right conclusion.

I asked him to look again at the three different groups. I commented that both people and animals eat, and sleep, and have babies while plants and minerals don't do any of those things. When I was certain that I had helped him see that people are part of the animal group, I asked the question again.

Immediately, Christopher answered that people do not belong to any of those groups. This was followed by more explaining on my part and more trying to help him see the obvious. Finally, after numerous attempts by me to help him come to the "right" conclusion, I told him that the answer was "animals. People are part of the group of animals."

Christopher remained unconvinced. "No, they're not," he replied. "People are not any of these things. They are something different. They are in a group all by themselves."

The light came on in *my* head! I realized that he was right. I had always held a strict Biblical Creationist worldview; yet, I had been so indoctrinated by my own public education that, without hesitation, I had agreed that people are animals.

I told him that he was absolutely right. We talked about how people are God's special creation and that they are in a group all by themselves. I then told him that they really just wanted to know which of these things people are most like, and he answered, "animals."

Example 2: When Stefan was seven or eight years old, he had this geography question, "If the world were made of glass, and you could look straight down and see through it, do you know what you would see?" The point of the question was to help the student understand that China is on the opposite side of the globe, and he would see China.

The question was hardly out of my mouth when Stefan replied, "Of course." I was certain that he did not know that in this scenario he would see China; therefore, I told him that I wanted him to think about his answer for a minute. I then asked the question again, and he instantly replied, "Of course."

I realized that I was going to get nowhere with this line of questioning so I said, "Okay. What would you see?"

"Hell," came the immediate response.

"Oh, yes, you would," I responded. I then told him that the point of the geography lesson was for him to understand that China was on the other side of the world. I then told him to imagine that we could move Hell out of the way so that he could see straight through to the other side. Then he would see China.

Example 3: Of course, sometimes a student is just hung up on an answer that really is wrong. When she was small, Victoria was convinced that we lived *inside* the earth. No matter how much I talked to her about gravity pulling us toward the center of the earth, she remained convinced that if we were really on the surface of the earth we would fall off. She maintained that the sky was the ceiling that served as the force that kept us inside. It took me a long time to convince her otherwise.

Example 4: Sometimes the "wrong" answer and the "right" answer are one in the same. One Saturday we were all watching a Rambo movie on television when one of the boys who was about eight years old said, "I know before I say this that when I do, everyone is going to say, 'You're crazy!' but, I think Rocky and Rambo look exactly alike." If my memory serves me correctly, most of his siblings accommodated him by assuring him that he was, indeed, "crazy" because he hadn't known that Rocky and Rambo were played by the same person.

It is a mother's job to keep everyone's self-esteem intact, and I told him that he was very clever to have recognized that Rocky and Rambo are the same person. He felt better.

Keep Your Students in the Classroom

On July 4, 1978, we moved into a house in Southern New Mexico's farming area. The house sits on half an acre among cotton fields and pecan orchards. Although the residence needed extensive renovation, it had a twenty-three by thirteen foot room that overlooked the backyard. Because the outside wall was comprised entirely of windows, it gave us a classroom with a twenty-three foot window on the world. John and I purchased a twelve foot long oak table and twelve chairs, and that room became our dining/schoolroom.

While the room was pleasant, and we witnessed many wonderful sights from our vantage point at the table, the day came quickly enough when the older children would have preferred completing their assignments in their bedrooms, or the family room, or the living room, or just about anywhere other than the schoolroom. With one exception, I insisted that all assignments be completed in the schoolroom.

As my students grew older, I allowed a child who had a long reading assignment to go to one of the other rooms to complete the reading portion of that assignment. He then returned to the schoolroom to complete the written portion. I felt that this was fair since with so many students, someone was always asking a question or I was giving one of them instructions, and the talking could be distracting. Even with this arrangement, however, most of the children chose to read at the table.

Part of the necessary discipline of a homeschool lies in having a designated place to complete assignments. If your students know that when they enter a particular room at a particular time they are "in school", their demeanor changes when they walk through the door. During those school hours they are no longer at home. They are in school. Everything that happens in that room during school hours is separate from their everyday lives. This is not the place to eat, or sleep, or watch television, or talk on the phone. When the school day ends, the room magically transforms back into the dining room, or the sun porch or the kitchen, but, until then, this is the place to learn.

The Best Laid Plans...

However carefully we plan, sooner or later we will be broadsided by something totally unexpected that will disrupt our homeschools. We all deal with the normal colds/flu/stomach viruses that take one or two of our students out of school for a day or two, but sometimes something occurs that threatens our very existence as homeschooling families.

On Thanksgiving Day, 1980, when Israel, my seventh child, was 14 months old, he experienced a condition known as intussusception, in which part of the bowel is pushed up inside of itself. This is commonly referred to as "telescoping" of the intestine. The result was that the various pediatricians on call kept telling me that Israel had the stomach flu, and by the time he was properly diagnosed five days later, gangrene had set in.

The night before Israel was properly diagnosed I sat up all night holding and rocking him. I knew that he was dying, and nobody would help me. We had excellent insurance and a pediatrician who had treated my children for nine years and was considered to be among the best in El Paso. Yet, I could not convince anyone to help. I was told numerous times by numerous doctors on call that Israel wasn't "nearly as sick as he seems to be."

By Sunday night I was so exhausted that I could not even continue to pray. I just sat rocking him and repeating the name of Jesus over and over. I was only five weeks away from giving birth to my eighth child, so I was not only emotionally drained, I was feeling the physical strain as well.

The next morning I told my husband that I was going to our pediatrician's office—he had now returned from his holiday and was seeing patients again—and that he was going to put Israel into the hospital. John also thought that I was over-reacting, but he agreed that if I felt that was the best course of action, I should go ahead and do it.

I was stunned when, after the doctor had examined Israel in his office, he told me to dress him. He then reiterated that Israel wasn't nearly as sick as he appeared to be and that he would be fine. I just stared at the doctor and silently prayed that God would open his eyes. The doctor then began to tick off Israel's symptoms: vomiting, stomach pain, diarrhea, etc. I turned to him and said, "I want everyone to stop saying that Israel has diarrhea. I have told everyone that

I have talked to that he does not have diarrhea. He has not had any bowel movements at all since early Thursday morning." I saw a light come on in the doctor's eyes, and he told me to undress Israel again. He then did a rectal exam and determined the real problem.

The doctor called ahead to the hospital and had a nurse waiting for me. Within a short time the pediatric surgeon appeared and performed the surgery during which he removed several inches of Israel's intestine. Israel was very sick, but he was in the hospital for only one week and made a quick recovery.

Although I had to suspend school for the week that I stayed at the hospital with Israel, we were soon back on our schedule.

Ten months later, in early October I gave the children their dinner, and they settled down in front of the television. Suddenly, Israel, who had celebrated his second birthday on September 26, walked over to me and said that his stomach hurt. That statement was followed by severe projectile vomiting. I was shocked, but I had learned from his previous intussusception that projectile vomiting is a symptom of an intestinal blockage. I was determined that we were not going to go through the delays in having him diagnosed that we had experienced the year before, and I told John that we had to take him to the emergency room immediately.

When we arrived at the emergency room, I told the ER doctor about Israel's history and directed him to call Dr. Rodriguez, the pediatric surgeon. I knew that Israel needed surgery, and I wanted to spare him as much suffering as possible.

The emergency room doctor called Dr. Rodriguez, who ordered some tests to determine whether there was another intestinal blockage. The tests came back negative. The doctor on duty in the emergency room told me that Israel had a stomach virus and not to worry about it.

I was only half convinced, but we took him home. That night Israel was in so much pain that I could hardly hold him on the bed. He continued to have projectile vomiting and screamed and rolled on the floor whenever he could escape from my arms.

The following morning I was at the pediatrician's office before he opened. Surely, considering what had happened the previous year, he would determine immediately that Israel had another blockage.

After a long wait, the doctor finally saw us. He was very annoyed and told me that this time Israel actually did have a stomach virus. Although I never raised my voice, he said that I was hysterical. He also said that he guessed that every time Israel vomited I was going to think that he had another blockage. He was extremely rude and let me know that he considered me to be wasting his time.

I just sat in his office, refusing to leave, and he finally told me that he was going to send us to the hospital. The doctor said that he was not going to have Israel admitted but that he would order an IV to hydrate him because he was "a little dry." Afterwards I would have to take him home. He then informed me that as soon as Israel had some fluids in him he would "perk right up."

I was very relieved to be going to the hospital because I thought that once inside I would be able to get someone to help me. The nurse was waiting for us, and she immediately started an IV. As soon as the IV was in place she left the room. I was sitting in a chair with Israel on my lap. He did not "perk right up." He stopped reacting to the pain and became more and more listless. After a few minutes I buzzed for the nurse, and when she appeared I said, "My child is dying, and no one will help me. I want you to call Dr. Rodriguez and tell him to come to the hospital because Israel's intestine is blocked."

The nurse looked at Israel carefully and said, "Yes, he is dying." She then told me that since my pediatrician had been the admitting doctor, she could not call the surgeon without his permission. She called my pediatrician and told him that Israel was turning gray and asked if she could give him some oxygen. The pediatrician replied, "Give him anything you want to. There's nothing wrong with that kid."

When the oxygen mask was in place, Israel pulled it off and said, "Jesus" loudly and clearly. I put the mask back in place, and the second time he pulled it off and said, "Jesus." Again I put the mask in place, and a third time he pulled it off and said, "Jesus." Then he lost consciousness.

The nurse told me that our pediatrician had called Dr. Rodriguez and that he would be coming to the hospital to see Israel. It was about noon when the call was made, but Dr. Rodriguez did not arrive until four-thirty that afternoon. When he saw Israel, he was stunned. Our pediatrician had told him that there was no emergency and that he should just drop by after office hours.

Dr. Rodriguez immediately called in a group of pediatricians who dealt with high risk children, and in less than an hour six specialists had formed a circle around Israel's bed. His abdomen was so distended that it measured thirty inches, and his vital signs were weak.

The medical team determined that Israel was now too weak to survive surgery and that they needed to stabilize him first. After several more hours they decided that he was going to die if they did not do the surgery. Finally, with Israel's condition having deteriorated considerably so that he was much less stable than when they had arrived, they operated.

Afterwards, the surgeon told John and me that we should prepare for Israel's death because he wasn't going to make it! Ultimately, Israel had surgery twice in thirty-six hours, and the surgeon removed about eighteen inches of his intestine.

It was after midnight when I left the hospital after that first surgery—John stayed so that he would be with Israel when he came out of recovery and was taken to his room. I wanted to stay too, but John insisted that I go home so that I could come back in the morning and relieve him.

On the thirty-minute drive home, I decided that I could finally allow myself the luxury of crying. I had forced myself to remain focused in the hours before and during the surgery, and my whole body was tense with the strain. I was alone in the dark car driving down a nearly deserted Interstate 10. This was the perfect time to let go. I was prepared to sob to my heart's content. I even screwed up my face in anticipation of what was to come.

Suddenly, I felt foolish. I certainly *could* have cried, but I realized that I did not *want* to cry. I knew that Israel was not only going to live but that he was going to return to perfect health. God had spared him, and God was going to heal him. Crying would have been a waste of salt water.

John and I were under enormous stress, and we were physically exhausted. Because we had no extended family living near us, we recruited whatever friends and acquaintances we could to babysit for the children at home during the day.

We missed about three weeks of school while I stayed at the hospital with Israel during the day and John stayed with him at night. The day after I brought Israel home, however, school resumed. For the first few weeks, unless he was napping, I held him on my lap while I taught the other children.

Israel's little body was so thin from his illness that he looked like a concentration camp victim. Fortunately, his appetite was good, but he was somewhat restricted in what he could eat. He was not allowed to have any dairy or orange juice for several months. Because he disliked all drinks other than milk, orange juice, and water, he drank only water. The foods he craved were canned tuna fish in vegetable oil, chicken, peanut butter, and brown sugar. I bought him his own jar of peanut butter and allowed him to eat it with a spoon directly out of the jar whenever he wished. From time to time I also gave him a little brown sugar in a cup. He ate entire cans of tuna fish with nothing on it other than the oil in which it was packed. Since he preferred dark meat, I bought chicken thighs in packages of six and simmered them so that the meat was very tender. One day after his nap he sat on my lap and ate all six of the chicken thighs that I had prepared while he was asleep.

Israel gained weight and grew stronger, but he was still very sick. His eyes looked dull and lifeless, and he had very little energy. I prayed for him constantly and recruited everyone I knew to pray for him too. John and the children were praying for him daily, and they finally became so exasperated with me that they just wanted me to stop asking for prayer.

Nevertheless, I continued to make a nuisance of myself. Frequently, when the whole family was together, I would place Israel on my lap and ask everyone to lay hands on him and pray for his healing. Everyone cooperated, but they did not understand my urgency. The doctor had said that if everything went well, by the time Israel was a teenager he would be able to participate in some sports and lead a somewhat normal life. John and the children thought that I should be grateful for such an optimistic prognosis. I was grateful, but I was not satisfied. I wanted Israel to bubble over with laughter; I wanted his eyes to sparkle with health; I wanted him to run and play and be filled with joy. I simply could not settle for less.

One evening nine months after his surgery I put Israel to bed and settled down to watch television with John and the older children. We turned on *The 700 Club*, and before long Pat Robertson said that he was going to pray for people with stomach and intestinal problems. I knew that this was the moment I had been waiting for. I was not a fan of either *The 700 Club* or Pat Robertson, but I was absolutely certain that Israel would be healed when Pat Robertson prayed.

I ran to Israel's bedroom and picked him up out of his crib and carried him into the family room where I lay him on the carpet in front of the television. Once again, I asked John and the children to lay hands on him and agree for his healing. They did so, but mostly, I think, to humor me. When Pat Robertson had finished his prayer, I lifted Israel up off the floor and carried him back to his bed without his ever having awakened.

I was thrilled! "Israel has been healed!" I announced.

"I really hope so," John replied, "because you are driving everyone crazy."

My enthusiasm was not dampened by his remark. I *knew* that in those few moments spent in prayer everything had changed. I knew that Israel was going to live a normal life from that day forward, and he did.

When he awakened the next morning, his eyes were bright and he looked healthy. A friend of ours happened to come by the house that day to talk to John. Manny did not believe in healing, and we had not shared anything with him about all of the prayers for Israel. When he saw Israel, however, Manny's eyes widened. "Every time I looked at him I could see Death in his eyes," Manny told us, "but it's gone.

He has life in him. What happened to him?" It was the right time for John to share the testimony of Israel's healing that had occurred less than twenty-four hours earlier.

A few weeks later, when I took Israel back to his pediatrician for his monthly examination, the doctor had a similar response. He stopped in the doorway to the examining room and asked me what had happened to Israel.

"He's well," I responded.

"I can see that," the doctor said. "How did he get that way?" It was my turn to witness about Israel's miracle.

After completing his examination, the pediatrician told me that I did not need to bring Israel back for subsequent follow-up visits. Throughout his childhood Israel remained healthy and vigorous.

It's Always Something

Fast forward to May 5, 1995. It was three-thirty on a Friday afternoon, and I had just come home from buying the weekly groceries. I had an interview scheduled with a radio station in Denver for four-thirty. They were supposed to call a little after four to get the phone hook-up in place for the interview. As I pulled into the driveway, I looked at my watch and congratulated myself that I had plenty of time to put the groceries away before the station called. I got out of the van to open the gate so that I could drive through, and the next thing I knew I was under the van rolling over and over thinking, "I would never have believed that this is the way I'm going to die."

The van, which held no other occupants, had begun to move forward and had run over me. Although I was alone when the accident happened, two of my sons found me there unconscious, and my husband backed the van off me while they pulled me out. When the pressure of the van was removed from my body, I began to breathe and regained consciousness, but I was badly hurt. My right leg had been wrapped around my neck and my right femur was broken completely through in two places and had been pushed out of my body under my hip. My right hip was broken, my pelvis was broken from top to bottom on both sides, and all but two of my ribs were broken. My lungs had been injured so badly that the entire time I was in the hospital I was given oxygen.

Just before I lost consciousness, I prayed and told God that if He didn't send someone to find me, I was going to die under that van. I then reminded Him that I really needed to finish raising my children. The next thing I knew my son Christopher was pulling me free, and I was breathing. I knew that I was going to live; God had sent someone to find me, and He wasn't going to let me die. Although I suffered horribly for months, I never once thought that I might die. It had all been settled under that van.

I have two rods in my right leg that extend to my knee—one on each side of the femur. I have never made a complete recovery, but I do not limp, and I am able to live a normal life. I am so very grateful that I was granted the time to raise my children and see my grandchildren, but my accident was more difficult to cope with than almost anyone could ever know.

I was uninsured at the time of my accident and, therefore, was a patient at the county hospital. Fortunately for me, because it is a teaching hospital it provides good quality physician care. Nevertheless, the nursing care and physical therapy are definitely substandard. During my hospitalization I had no more than three physical therapy sessions, and those did not involve any real therapy. I was very worried about how I would be able to get my leg back in shape.

On the day that I was released from the hospital I was told that I could not have any physical therapy after my release. The nurse gave me a tight-lipped little smile and said, "We are sending you home with no medications, not even an antibiotic."

I was still running a temperature and in such poor physical condition that I did not know how I was going to cope. The panic that I experienced was almost uncontrollable; I wanted to start screaming at the top of my lungs. Instead, I just nodded my head and kept my mouth tightly closed. As I sat alone in a wheelchair in the hallway while John went to the office to complete the paperwork for my release, I prayed. I told God that I was putting myself in His hands and trusting Him for my recovery.

After that, I never looked back. I thought about what I wanted to do. "I want to walk," I told myself. "The best therapy to learn to walk again is probably just to walk." Walking became my focus. I was never going to ice skate or ski or compete in the Olympics—I had never done any of those things before, and at age fifty it was unlikely that, even under the best circumstances, I would start then. I needed to direct my energy towards real goals that I could expect to achieve.

While I was in the hospital, the older children had each "adopted" one of the younger ones to teach. The older children were employed full-time, but when they came home from work, they set their respective students down and checked on their progress. I was so ill that I could not even think about school, but they kept the school going entirely independently of me.

My first day home Israel brought me an assignment he had prepared to send to Cal State as part of his Master's degree program. It was a ten-page paper, typewritten, double-spaced. He asked me to read it and let him know what I thought. To my horror, when I tried to read the paper, I did not understand anything it said! I recognized all of the words, but it was gibberish to me. I spent the entire day trying to read that paper and never got beyond the first paragraph.

The day I had my accident the doctors had informed my family that I would suffer some brain damage. Because I had been oxygen deprived for an undetermined length of time, they did not know to what extent I might be affected, but they said that the effects could range from my being a "vegetable" to being mildly impaired. My family had shared this information with me while I was in the hospital, and at that time it seemed that I had suffered no ill effects from the oxygen deprivation.

When I was faced with reading Israel's assignment, however, I knew that I was going to have to work to overcome whatever damage had been done. I did not tell anyone that I could not read the paper until months later. At the end of the day I called Israel into my room, handed the assignment back to him and said, "I think it's fine. Go ahead and mail it."

Because I was sent home from the hospital without any medications, I knew that drugs were not playing a part in my inability to understand what I was reading. I was certain, however, that my condition was temporary and that I would soon not only be reading but comprehending as well as ever.

A few days later, I told the children who were still in school to bring their school materials into my bedroom, and I worked with them from my bed. The youngest was twelve, and all who were still in school were earning either their undergraduate or graduate degrees. After a few days, I dragged myself into my wheelchair and went into the school room. I was so weak and in so much pain that I felt as if every cell in my body was on fire. While the children completed their school work, I lay my head on the table because I was too weak to hold it upright for more than a few minutes.

Although it was a typical blazing-hot El Paso summer, I experienced a strange phenomenon that lasted for about three months. Every morning at exactly eleven o'clock I experienced horrible chills. I wrapped myself in a big comforter, but I was so cold that I virtually shook all over. My temperature would rise to between 102 and 103 degrees, and I would remain in this state until two p.m. My temperature would then return to normal and I would begin perspiring. Afterwards I remained free of these symptoms for twenty-four hours, but I always knew when eleven o'clock had arrived.

Alexandra was only twenty-four years old, and she was working full-time, but she took over the main responsibilities of running the household. In addition, she took the lead in caring for me. Many days the only thing I could ingest was grape juice. She was worried about me and tried hard to tempt me with some of my favorite foods.

We were so broke during this time. We had no money at all, but each week she bought limes to make limeade and avocados to make guacamole—not only for me but for the whole family. I was always able to enjoy this delicious weekly treat.

On weekends Alexandra insisted that I go for rides with her. Getting into the car was such an effort that I could hardly make myself do it, but it was an important part of my healing process. Although I was not allowed to put any weight on my right leg, I had progressed enough so that I could drag myself around the house in a walker while holding my right leg so that it never touched the floor. This allowed me to regain some strength, but I was a hostage inside my own house. Alexandra's insistence on those rides in the car brought me the fresh air and sunshine that proved to be an important part of my healing process.

Another important factor in my recovery was the goals that I set for myself. A primary concern was being able to cook Thanksgiving dinner for my family. My girls always helped with the cooking, but I wanted to be able to take the lead in the holiday preparations. The mobility that I gained from using my walker was an important component in reaching my goals.

I discovered that by putting objects such as my shampoo and conditioner in a plastic grocery bag, I could loop my fingers through the handle and hold onto my walker while holding the bag. Thus, I was able to drag myself around the house and get the things I needed without inconveniencing anyone.

I was soon making the bed and cleaning the refrigerator while standing on one foot and holding onto the walker with one hand. I sat at the table to make salads and prepare food for family meals. Even though I was limited in what I could do, I was able to constantly expand my activities by really thinking about how I could execute various tasks.

In late summer the doctor said that I could begin putting some weight on my right leg. That was a huge milestone. I was allowed to exert only limited pressure, but this helped enormously in allowing me to do more. I improvised a "track" inside the house which allowed me to move through an interior loop by using connecting rooms and hallways. Before long I had worked my way up to ten "laps" but, at first, the effort was exhausting.

In October the doctor told me that I could begin walking with a cane. Alexandra offered to buy me a pretty, feminine-looking one, but I refused. I told her that I was not going to use a cane very long and the ugly aluminum one that John had bought years earlier when he had injured his leg would do just fine. As it turned out, I used the cane for only ten days before I decided to toss it and force myself to learn to walk unaided.

Those first solo attempts were pathetic. My leg felt as heavy as lead, and I walked with a horrible limp. I was very embarrassed. I walked, and walked, and walked some more, but my limp was still severe. Finally, I asked the doctor why I was continuing to limp when I was making such an effort not to. He responded that my muscles were very weak and that every time I took a step my pelvis dropped on the right side. He said that unless I could strengthen those muscles sufficiently, I would never be able to walk without a limp.

On October 31, six months after my accident, the doctor gave me permission to begin driving, and I drove for the first time that day. To my surprise, I experienced no anxiety, either about driving in general or about the fact that I was driving the same van that had run over me.

I also accomplished my goal of preparing Thanksgiving dinner for my family. Thanksgiving was especially meaningful for me that year because I felt that I was well on my way to getting my life back.

About that time I found a new friend. Jenny went to the same church we did, and she lived only about a mile from us. Jenny was a few years younger than I, but her children were grown. She was really into exercise and was looking for someone to walk with her. She and I decided that each afternoon when I was finished with school we would go walking.

Jenny really pushed me, and she eventually had me walking four miles a day. She walked as fast as she could without losing me. I continued to make progress, and after a couple of years my muscles were strong enough so that I no longer limped.

In 1998 I drove the van to Provo, Utah, where Stefan and Judah took their Closure seminar at BYU and graduated. Since they were both far too young to drive, I did all of the driving myself. I also accomplished my goal of being able to wear high heels again. I wore a tailored suit and three-inch heels to their graduation banquet. I felt that I had graduated right along with them.

I am not saying that everyone should take as rigid an approach to homeschooling as I did. In retrospect, I think I was probably too hard on myself. However, homeschooling is a commitment that requires years of unwavering dedication. Through the many financial and physical obstacles that came our way, I learned that it was my responsibility to deal with whatever life brought and keep my homeschool intact and on schedule.

Whose Hand Wrote on the Wall?

Dealing with Your Preschoolers

When my daughter Victoria was five or six years old, I purchased a Bible Trivia game that I thought we would have fun playing together as a family. One afternoon as I sat reading questions from the cards to the children, I came across one that said, *"In Chapter 5 of the Book of Daniel, whose hand wrote on the wall?"* Victoria's eyes widened, and she instantly replied, "It wasn't mine!"

This incident clearly illustrates the struggle we had in our home with people writing and drawing on the walls. It seemed that no matter how much I lectured/punished the graffiti artists, they continued to use the walls as their canvases. I found crayon pictures and scribbles on the walls of the playroom, inside the bedroom closets and even inside dresser drawers. It did not matter that we kept a huge supply of drawing paper at all times. There was just no substitute for a freshly painted/washed wall.

Not long ago I was moving a beautiful bedside table that John and I had purchased in 1965 into our guest bedroom. It has an antique olive finish and is in perfect condition. I was congratulating myself that it had survived all of those years and all of those children and had emerged in like-new condition when I opened the top drawer. To my horror, the bottoms and sides of both drawers were covered with crayon scribbles in various shades of red, green, black, and blue!

Long after my crayon-on-the-walls days were history, an exciting new invention emerged—the Mr. Clean Magic Eraser. By using it I was able to remove every trace of crayon from the wood interiors of the drawers, and now my bedside table really is like new. The experience, however, reminded me that keeping up with my preschoolers was a full-time job.

For homeschooling mothers, dealing with preschoolers while they are in the classroom can be a real challenge. There is no fail safe method for ensuring that you will have no mishaps, but by setting up some simple guidelines, you can prevent most disasters.

Since I had preschoolers for many years, I had to learn how to cope with them from the very beginning. By adopting a few simple guidelines for your preschoolers, you, too, can have a much less stressful homeschooling experience.

Establish Perimeters

The first thing that I did was to establish perimeters for the preschoolers. Children are very intelligent little people, and they are usually capable of a lot more than we think. I found that by setting up strict guidelines for my preschoolers, I was able to let them know exactly what was expected of them. Consequently, I was able to help them not to overstep their bounds.

The really little babies were easy. I either held them on my lap, or they napped. When Benjamin, my sixth child, was born, someone gave us a baby swing. One day when he was about five months old, I took the swing into the schoolroom to see whether he would enjoy sitting in it for a while. At eight-thirty I deposited him into the swing. Immediately his eyes glazed over, and he sat completely motionless as the rhythmic motion of the swing lulled him into a deep sleep. By eight-forty I was laying him in his crib where he slept soundly for the next several hours. We repeated this scenario every day for several months. The baby was sleeping, my lap was free, and life was good.

The older preschoolers presented more of a challenge. I always put the oldest preschooler in charge of the younger ones. I then told the one in charge that it was his responsibility to tell me immediately if any of the younger children did anything they were not supposed to do. I made it clear that he was not supposed to try to make the younger children behave. He was just supposed to tell me if they misbehaved.

I then told the younger children that if the one in charge did anything that he was not supposed to do, they were to tell me immediately. In that way everyone was responsible for making certain that no one was breaking the rules.

This arrangement worked well. The oldest preschooler gained the prestige of being "in charge" and took his position very seriously. The younger children liked the idea that if the one in charge stepped out of line they were to report on him. Everyone figured out pretty quickly that if they broke any rules, they were going to be caught right away. This gave them plenty of incentive to behave.

I cannot tell you how many bottles of shampoo were saved from being dumped down the toilets or how many tubes of toothpaste from being squeezed down the bathroom sink drains. I do know that because of this system most of our school days were fairly uneventful.

The second thing that I did was to let the preschoolers know what they might and might not do during school hours. Never say to a child, "Go play and don't bother us." You may as well hand him a loaded gun and a box of matches because what preschoolers consider harmless fun and what mothers consider harmless fun are seldom the same.

Every day before school began I took my preschoolers aside and reminded them of who was in charge. I then asked them, "What do you want to do while we are in school?" and I laid out the various options:

- They could watch a television program that I had approved.
- They could watch a tape on the VCR.
- They could play with toys in the playroom.
- They could come into the schoolroom and color or play with clay if they worked quietly and did not talk.
- They could bring a toy into the schoolroom if they played quietly.

Although the list of options was always the same, each day I asked the preschoolers what they wanted to do while we were in school. When I had their responses, I helped them get started on their chosen activities. I then told them that when they were ready to do something else, they were to come to the schoolroom and tell me so that I could get them started on their new activity.

This approach kept everyone focused, and we had surprisingly few mishaps. Yet, even with the most careful planning on my part, we did have some incidents that made me realize that their ideas about acceptable play did not line up with mine.

One day as I sat teaching my children, I heard the sound of metal clanking. It was not loud, but it was constant. Realizing that this could not be a good thing, I got up to investigate. I walked into the family room to find two and a half year old Israel and three and a half year old Benjamin having a "sword fight." Israel was armed with a large meat fork and Benjamin was brandishing a butcher knife.

I confiscated their weapons and sat them down for a talk. I told them that I was not going to spank them this time, but if they ever did it again, I was going to give both of them a spanking.

I knew that simply forbidding them to "sword fight" would never work, so I went to the cabinet where I kept the school supplies, found two wooden rulers that Calvert had sent with their program, and handed each boy a ruler. "You can sword fight with these," I said, "but these are the only swords you can use. If you use anything else, I am going to spank you. Do you understand?"

The boys nodded affirmatively and instantly resumed their sport. Although I instructed them to keep those rulers for sword fighting, from that day forward, no ruler in our house was safe. If the sword fighting urge happened to strike when a school box was nearer at hand than their designated weapons, Benjamin and Israel took rulers out of their older siblings' school boxes. As a result, every one of the several dozen rulers in our house was badly dinged, but from that day forward, the wooden Calvert ruler was the only weapon ever used for sword fighting. By the time our preschoolers were old enough to lose interest in sword fighting, most of our rulers were little more than really long splinters.

Years later, our neighbor's son married a woman who had been homeschooled through the Calvert program. Although she was in her late twenties, she still had one of her Calvert School rulers. This young lady, who was an only child, had kept her ruler in pristine condition.

When we were alone, John asked me why our children had been so "destructive" with their rulers when it was obvious that other Calvert students were able to preserve their school supplies so that they could be used well into adulthood. I just rolled my eyes.

Be Respectful

Never say to your preschoolers, "We are busy; leave us alone, and do not interrupt us." That is just rude, and nobody wants to be treated that way.

Imagine that one day you go to a friend's house for an impromptu visit. She opens the door, looks at you, and frowns. Just before she slams the door in your face she says, "I'm talking to someone else. Don't bother us. We're busy."

You would be hurt and embarrassed, and you would be so offended that you would probably never go to her house again. Yet, this is the way we sometimes treat our children. We react to them as if they are nuisances who do not deserve to be treated with the same respect we show adults.

Always keep the Golden Rule in mind when dealing with your children. Treat even the youngest member of your family with the respect and kindness you want others to show you. Children have the same emotions that you have. They feel the same hurt, anger, and humiliation as adults. Treat them with the respect that you demand they give you. Help them to feel included rather than excluded.

Your preschoolers are vitally important to the success of your homeschool. Every day let them know that you are counting on them. Tell them that you are proud of them for behaving so well; tell them that you appreciate their contributions. Never be afraid to tell them that their good behavior makes your homeschool possible. They will be proud of themselves for having played such an important role.

About once a month in the late afternoon I called all the children together. While everyone was present, I thanked each of them individually for something specific that he or she had done that month that had been a special help to me. For the very little children, their contribution was often that they had made me laugh or had made me feel loved, but when I listed their contributions, they felt just as special as the older children. It was a little thing, but I wanted them to know that I appreciated their contributions. It is a practice that I highly recommend to all homeschooling mothers.

A Woman's Work Is Never Done

Scheduling Your Housework

Having a clean, orderly house was always a high priority for me. In fact, before we had children John and I bought our first house and carpeted everything except the kitchen in off-white carpeting. The walls, drapes and carpet were the color of a pearl. I loved it, and other people were extremely complimentary as well. In fact, the only negative response we ever received about the appearance of our first home was that it was "too clean."

When we started having children and found it necessary to purchase a larger house, we were smart enough to opt for a color palate that was more kid-friendly, but I still wanted our home to be neat and clean. Keeping everything spiffy was not too difficult before I made the commitment to homeschool, but when I realized that for a sizeable chunk of my day I was going to be sequestered in my schoolroom, I knew that I was going to need to set up a schedule for my housework that would be as unbending as my school schedule.

As I began working out my schedule, I realized that in order to get everything done I needed to get up at five-thirty every morning. This was hard for me. I was always up at six, but losing that additional thirty minutes of sleep seemed like a huge sacrifice to me. Nevertheless, until my children were old enough to help me with household chores, I was going to have to haul myself out of bed at five-thirty a.m.

When I got out of bed, the first thing I did was put on my makeup and style my hair. When I was dressed, I went into the kitchen and started cooking breakfast.

I had time set aside on my schedule for everything that I would do during the day:

- A time to make the beds
- A time to do the laundry
- A time to wash the dishes
- A time to sweep the floors
- A time to vacuum
- A time to dust

Because I had scheduled everything that I would need to do during the day, I never really had an excuse for not doing something. I could never justify saying, "Oh, well, I think I'll let that go today," because I knew each task had a time slot when it was supposed to be completed.

This may sound like a grueling life, but the schedule made it possible for me to spend the required time in school and complete my housework every day. Of course, in order for the schedule to be effective, I had to actually discipline myself to follow it, and this is where that thing called "habit" came into play. The word "habit" tends to carry with it a negative connotation. We attribute all sorts of unsavory behavior to bad habits, but we seldom attribute positive behavior to good habits. Yet, our habits dictate most of our lives. Each of us has bad habits and good habits; the key to success in any endeavor lies in minimizing our bad habits and maximizing our good habits.

Those who study such things have said that without habits we would be unable to function. We tie our shoelaces, button our shirts, or put on our socks with ease because we have formed habits that allow us to perform these tasks without giving them much thought.

I once read that when people brush their teeth, they begin at the same spot in their mouths each time and work around their mouths in the same pattern. While each of us has developed his own tooth brushing habit that may differ somewhat from another person's tooth brushing habit, each time we brush our teeth, we do it exactly the same way. We do this unconsciously because we have spent so many years reinforcing this particular habit.

Can you imagine getting up every morning and having to decide how you were going to brush your teeth? "Which tooth do I brush first? Which side do I start on? Do I begin with the upper teeth or the lower teeth?" The possibilities are endless, and without the benefit of habit, brushing your teeth would become a very time-consuming chore.

By doing things in the same order every day I formed habits that helped me finish my housework quickly and efficiently. I never had to wonder when I was going to find time to perform a particular chore; I knew exactly when I was going to do everything because everything was on the schedule. Thus, performing the mundane household tasks that are an inescapable part of life became a habit. I no longer gave any thought to when or how I was going to perform any of my duties. I followed the schedule and developed habits that enabled me to complete my housework quickly.

Make Work Assignments Permanent

When the children were old enough to begin helping with chores, I wanted them to have the benefit of habit in completing their assigned tasks. In order to accomplish this, I gave permanent work assignments. I do not know of anyone else who does this, but it works beautifully, and I recommend it highly.

I have been in many homes where the work assignments rotate. It is my opinion, however, that rotating work assignments creates several problems. The most obvious is that no one ever seems to be able to agree about whose week it is to do what. Even though the parents have put forth the effort to provide a written schedule showing everyone's work assignments for a particular week, the children never seem to accept the schedule as either fair or accurate. They often believe that their workload is bigger than their siblings' and that the rotation favors everyone but them.

Another problem with rotating work assignments is that no one ever gets familiar enough with any particular task to take advantage of the role that habit plays in completing household chores. Although the children perform a variety of chores over a short period of time, they do not become really adept at completing any of their assignments. On the other hand, if children perform the same household tasks over an extended period of time, those tasks become second nature to them, and they are able to finish their chores more efficiently.

Include Everyone in the Chores

My mother often tells me that she gave me my first job when I was only two years old. It was my duty to stack the magazines that she kept on the coffee table. Mother loved to read magazines, and each month she purchased five or six. Those magazines were kept on the coffee table until she replaced them with their new issues.

Each morning it was my job to stack them in order of size with the largest on the bottom. Her magazines ranged in size from *Life*, which was huge, to *The Reader's Digest*, which was quite small. I have only a vague memory of stacking those magazines, but I now realize that for a two year old that was, undoubtedly, a challenging task; I must have struggled to get the order right.

Perhaps, that early experience helped give me an appreciation of the role that habit plays in making our lives easier. I am certain that over time habit made it much easier for me to complete that simple chore.

Stacking those magazines probably also made me aware that even the youngest child can accept responsibility for some household chores. For instance, a two year old can bring his mother a clean diaper when she is changing the baby; he can also put away his toys. The key is finding tasks that a two year old can actually complete.

Putting away the toys was the first job that my children learned. Of course, I could not just say to a two year old, "Put away your toys." That would have been tantamount to handing him a message written in hieroglyphics and expecting him to follow the instructions.

Each time the children finished playing with their toys, they were required to put them away. That meant that we spent a lot of time during the day just putting away toys. One of the boys' bedrooms was also the playroom, and, normally, the toys were confined to that room. Even though the toys were in their designated play area, when it was time to do something else for a while, the toys had to be put away.

When the children were very small, I would enter the room and tell them that it was time to put away the toys. I would then point at each individual toy and tell a child to put that toy in the toy box. As each toy was deposited into the toy box, I would point at another toy and give the same instruction until everything had been put away. Of course, this method was very slow; I could have done the job myself in a fraction of the time. However, if I had done so, they would not have learned to put away the toys; they would have learned that Mom puts away the toys.

As the children grew older, I could simply say, "Ok, Kiddos, it's time to put away the toys." The older ones would begin working, and I was left to point at toys for the younger children. Thus, the process was considerably expedited.

Eventually, the younger children became so eager to imitate their older siblings that I no longer had to supervise.

They, too, took toys to the toy box because they wanted to fit in. At that point, I could actually go to the door and say, "Ok, Kiddos, it's time to put away the toys."

Spend Time Training Your Children for Their Chores

Erma Bombeck once said, "Housework done properly will kill you." While her statement is probably an exaggeration, housework sometimes has the ability to make you wish you were dead. I can think of no better reason to insist that your children accept some of the responsibility for maintaining a clean, orderly home.

If, however, this division of duties is going to meet with any success, Mom must spend time training each child for each household task he is expected to perform. When I was training my children, I began by performing a particular task while the trainee watched. For instance, when I was training my daughter to clean the bathrooms, I spent a couple of weeks cleaning the bathrooms while I talked about everything I was doing. "This is how we clean the tub. This is how we clean the chrome; this is how we clean the mirror." As I cleaned each item, I discussed the techniques and products that we used for each.

After a couple of weeks, I told my daughter that she was to clean the bathrooms on her own and that when she finished the first one she was to call me so that I could inspect her work. I naively believed that when she called I would be greeted with a room filled with snowy porcelain and gleaming chrome. When I heard the much anticipated, "Mom, I'm ready," I was stunned to enter door number one to find a considerable amount of green Comet powder covering every object. Francesca was beaming with pride over what she considered to be a perfectly executed job, and I, of course, did not want to burst her bubble.

"That's great!" I said. "But there are a few things we still need to work on." I then rinsed off the Comet while we talked about how to make everything "even better." Although the training process took quite a while, the final result was well worth the effort. Francesca learned to clean bathrooms with a precision mastered by few young people, and she was able to complete her work in a short time.

A couple of years later I began to feel guilty because she had to clean four bathrooms each day, and I asked her whether she would like to change her job assignment. She replied, "No, I can clean these bathrooms really fast, and I'm keeping this job!"

Training your children takes time and patience. You have to stick it out with them. You have to call them back and say, "This part isn't done right. Redo this and then call me." Then you have to go back and inspect again, but after a while they learn their jobs.

Whether it was dusting and polishing the furniture or washing the dishes, every job required a training process. In the end, however, those hours spent training the children proved to be some of the most valuable I ever spent. What might have killed me only made me tired.

How Permanent Is Permanent?

Permanent and *forever* are not synonyms: "permanent press" does sometimes wrinkle, "permanent ink" will eventually fade or disappear completely, and hair that has been processed with a "permanent wave" will, in time, become straight and limp.

Keeping this in mind, we might rephrase "permanent" work assignments to say that the work assignments were "permanent until further notice." Obviously, as children grow and mature, they are able to take on more responsibility and more complicated tasks. When they "outgrow" their present assignments, they should be given ones that are more age appropriate.

In addition, all families experience "job openings" for a variety of reasons. When our older children began to work outside the home, most of their work was turned over to the children who were home all day. Because of the natural maturation of the younger siblings, no one ever had an unreasonable workload, and everyone always had age appropriate work assignments.

Although it was our policy that when someone had been assigned a particular job it was going to belong to him for several years, I did try to be considerate of the children's feelings. When Dominic was about ten or eleven, I made it his job to fold the laundry and place each person's folded clothing on his bed. I always did all of the washing and drying of the laundry, so he was responsible only for the folding and delivery.

After the first day Dominic came to me and asked that he be given a different job. He said that he would be willing to take two harder jobs to replace that one if I would not make him fold the laundry. When I asked him why he was so opposed to what seemed to me to be a pretty easy job, he told me that he was very embarrassed to have to fold "women's underwear." He had four sisters, but it had never occurred to me that folding their clothes might be a problem for him. I immediately gave him one job that was equally challenging and excused him from folding clothes permanently. After that, I never asked any of the boys to fold clothes; that became "women's work." I have always wondered, though, why girls are not embarrassed to fold men's underwear.

The final benefit of permanent work assignments is that if something is not done properly or not done at all, you know exactly who is to blame. It is pretty difficult for a child to make the argument that he did not know that he was supposed to do something when that particular job has been his responsibility for a year or two. Your children know that there is no possibility that they will be able to squirm out of their work, so they tend to get busy and finish quickly. This makes life easier for both you and them.

It's Not Just Another Name for Housework

Scheduling Your Homework

I still remember how liberated I felt a few days before my high school graduation. I was a very good student and the salutatorian of my graduating class. Besides, I loved learning and was interested in a variety of subjects that could have led to careers in various fields. Nevertheless, I knew that I would not be going to college. I had, therefore, taken every business course available in high school so that I could find work as a secretary as soon as I graduated.

Thus, as I approached my high school graduation, I felt a level of exhilaration that can only be explained by the knowledge that I was FINISHED WITH SCHOOL. Never again would I have to open a textbook, or complete some inane assignment, or do the dreaded homework. I was FREE! Little did I know that twelve years later I would begin a homeschooling odyssey that would necessitate my being in school five days a week, twelve months a year, for twenty-five years. My commitment, however, would entail a great deal more than just sitting in the classroom for three or more hours a day teaching and testing my children. My decision to homeschool meant that I would need to spend many evenings and weekends studying and preparing so that those classroom hours with my students would progress smoothly.

Homeschooled Children Never Have Homework

It is one of the pleasant realities of homeschooling that the children do not have homework. At our house everything was completed during those three hours spent in the classroom each day. The children could leave school knowing that afternoons, evenings, and weekends were theirs to spend as they wished.

I do not believe that they will ever be able to appreciate what an advantage that gave them over children who attended public or private schools. They played outside or read or watched television without ever having to give a thought to the following day's lessons. When school was over for the day, it was really OVER for the day.

I believed that since the children had so much structure in their school, their free time should be as unstructured as possible. Because they were on a strict schedule as far as their household chores and school was concerned, I did not interfere with their play time. As a result, they learned to be wonderfully creative in inventing their own games and doing the things they enjoyed best. For several years an ordinary swing set became a "covered wagon" in which they were moving west. They passed many happy hours as a family of pioneers making the trek to settle new territories.

They also invented a game called "Thin Air Football." They enjoyed this game for months before I realized how it was played. One day as I looked out the kitchen window while preparing dinner, I observed a heated argument complete with shouting, red faces, and flailing arms. The oldest children were probably about ten and eleven years old at that time, and they had divided their siblings into two teams with each team headed by one of the older children. I finally decided that they were not going to resolve this conflict in a peaceful way, so I went to the door and asked them what was going on.

I was told that they were playing football but they were arguing because they played it with a "thin air ball." It seemed that all of the arguing stemmed from a disagreement over who had possession of the ball. "Where is the ball?" I asked.

"We don't have a ball, it's a thin air ball," I was told. "That's why we're fighting. It's hard to tell who has the ball when it's thin air."

I was immediately overcome with guilt. My children wanted to play football so much that they were playing it even though they did not have a ball! Until that moment I had not realized that they did not own a football. I was sure that I must be the worst mother in the world.

The next day I went to Wal-Mart and bought a football. I beamed as I presented it to them, and I imagined that they would now pass their afternoons in peaceful bliss as they played "real" football. To my dismay the ball went into the closet and, until the boys were much older, they never played football again—either "thin air" or "real." In my zeal to make their game better, I had ruined it for them. They actually *liked* not having a football. It was only the "thin air" aspect of the game that had made it fun!

Homeschooling Mothers Always Have Homework

The rules for homeschooling mothers are very different from those of homeschooled children. While my children were enjoying lives free from homework, I was a virtual homework machine. I read every textbook that was assigned for our homeschool. Keeping up with the work in the lower grades was challenging, but when the children reached undergraduate and graduate work, my study time exploded. During some years I read between forty and fifty textbooks.

I knew that in order to mentor them I would have to be thoroughly prepared, and that meant that I must immerse myself in the curricula. In order to be able to help them with difficulties they might encounter as they progressed through their lessons, I needed to understand every subject that they would be learning. I discussed every assignment with them and read every paper they ever wrote. When they took algebra and geometry, I worked through their assignments the night before so that if they encountered a problem the following day in school, I could immediately find their mistake and show them where it was. I then had them go back to that point, make that correction, and finish the problem.

I was fortunate in that all of the children used the same schools and the same curricula. Consequently, it was necessary for me to read and study the books from Alexandra's courses, but I did not have to continue to read the younger children's books. Of course, every now and then, an old familiar text was retired and a new one introduced. At those times I had to start over with my reading.

Obviously, a certain amount of preparation had to be done by just sitting down and doing it, but I found that there are many little pockets of time that occur in every life that can be used constructively if we are prepared to take advantage of them.

For years I walked around with a textbook in my hand—it was as if it had grown to my fingers. I never went anywhere without a textbook. If there were a doctor's or dentist's appointment, I carried my book with me. When I met my husband at a restaurant for our Friday night "date", I took a textbook so that I could read while I waited for him. Every minute spent waiting for my appointments was a minute spent preparing. Even when Israel was so ill in the hospital, I spent those three weeks at the hospital holding him on my lap while I read textbooks.

I learned that by taking advantage of five minutes here and ten or fifteen minutes there, at the end of the day those minutes amounted to a considerable amount of time. If I had not used those little pockets of time to study, they would have been wasted moments which I would have spent doing little more than staring into space.

Did I have to study during the evening? As a famous female Governor of Alaska once said, "You betcha!" However, I learned to study in the evenings without isolating myself from the rest of the family. I have always been able to shut out everything around me and focus on reading material. I was, therefore, able to sit with my family while they watched television or played board games and do my homework while they enjoyed themselves.

When Is a Dinner Table Not a Dinner Table?

As the children entered university and graduate work I found the dinner table discussion to be an extremely valuable tool. I mentioned earlier that when school is in session, the schoolroom can never serve any other purpose. However, when the family gathers for the evening meal, the dinner table may become both dinner table and think tank. Because there are so many concepts to be discussed in philosophy, history and literature courses, it can be difficult to find time for in-depth discussions of the subject matter.

Therefore, nearly every evening was spent discussing various assigned texts that one of my students had read. As we talked informally, they never felt that they were being grilled. I could ask about their insights into certain aspects of the material, and they were able to answer without feeling the pressure of being "wrong". In addition, the other children who had already completed those courses added their perspectives. The dinner table discussion gave us an opportunity to explore topics in a great deal more depth than would have been possible if the exchange of ideas had been limited to a classroom session between the student and me.

The possibilities for using "wasted moments" are almost unlimited. Whether riding in the car, taking a walk, or just enjoying each other's company, the opportunity for an informal discussion of something your students are studying in school is always with you. As the teacher you will know whether they are on the wrong track, and you can help them correct any misconceptions. In addition, with everyone contributing to the discussion, you will find that a number of insights are coming into play that will give the target student a much better grasp of the material than he would have on his own. An added benefit is that the younger children hear the material discussed before they ever encounter it. This gives them a small foundation to build on when they are presented with those texts. You will be amazed by how much this practice helps your younger students become familiar with the books they will be required to read later.

After Alexandra finished school, we were faced with the dilemma of what to do with a sixteen year old who had a master's degree. Ultimately, she would begin teaching college history at age eighteen, but we had a gap of about eighteen months when she needed to be occupied. She was an enormous help to me with the house and the homeschool. She began helping me teach the younger children, and that was great, but I wanted her to have something that was hers, so I suggested that she spend some of her time writing a book about her homeschooling experiences. The result was *No Regrets: How Homeschooling Earned me a Master's Degree at Age Sixteen.* The book sold out two printings and was out of print for quite a while, but in April of 2010 we rereleased it.

Alexandra is an excellent writer and needed very few suggestions, but before she began writing, she and I went for a walk at the farm where we kept our horses. We are in southern New Mexico, and the scenery is very different from that of most of the United States. The treeless mountains are rugged and purple. Sand dunes and desert plants dominate the landscape, and the sky is like a hot blue lid that presses the heat down on all who venture out of doors. After the summer rains wild flowers spring up in various shades of yellow and lavender. It is wild, untamed and beautiful.

As we walked down a dirt road, I pointed out the various sights. We talked about the incredible beauty of the natural landscape, and then I asked her a question. If we were going to paint a picture of this, what would we leave out? We finally decided that we would leave out the telephone poles because they distracted from the experience. We also decided that we would leave out the tiny building in the distance because it was also a distraction. Then I pointed out a small clump of beautiful violet-colored wild flowers. "I would leave those out, too," I said, "because even though they are very beautiful, they are not representative of what we actually see on this walk, and if we were to focus on them, our picture would not really represent what we are experiencing today."

I then reminded her that a famous painter once said that when anyone paints a picture, he should leave out everything that does not help someone who views the picture to see what he as the artist sees. He went on to say that the mark of an amateur is to include everything in a painting; in doing so he produces a work that is highly unsatisfactory and unfocused. As a result, the person who views the artist's work is never able to share the experience that prompted him to create the painting in the first place.

My advice to her was, "This is not the story of your life; this is your story. Write about everything that contributes to that story. Tell about the sad things and the difficulties as well as the successes, but make certain that you do not get bogged down trying to write about every detail of your life. Write about the things that make up *your* story." She actually followed my advice and produced a wonderful narrative that has blessed many homeschooling families.

This summer a very prominent El Pasoan saw her at an event for the city and told her that when he and his wife were moving into their new house that Alexandra had just financed for them, he came across *No Regrets*. They had owned the book for many years, and he had known Alexandra for a while and done several mortgage transactions with her, but he had not realized that she was the same person who had authored the book until he ran across it while preparing to move. He told her that he was going to bring it by our offices for her to sign.

Homeschooling never really ends. You will always remain your children's teacher. Long after my children were grown and had good jobs they called me from work to ask me questions about grammar and spelling. One of my sons once called long distance from the television station in Kansas City where he was working to ask me how to spell a word. I gave him the correct spelling, and I refrained from asking, "Don't they have dictionaries at Fox?"

I believe that one of the greatest blessings any of us can experience is to be able to teach our children at home. Under no other circumstances can we know everything that our children are being taught and have an opportunity to hear their thoughts on so many different subjects. Homeschooling is a gift from God, and we need to remember that—even when we are tired, or sick, or discouraged. It provides a connection between us and our children that lasts a lifetime. They may not appreciate the sacrifices that we have made for them when they are teenagers and young adults, but they will eventually recognize that what we did, we did for love.

Train up a Child

What Does it Prosper a Man if He Gains the Whole World and Loses His Soul?

In the early 1970's we were friends with a wonderful Christian couple who were about 20 years older than I. The husband was a retired military chaplain, and the wife was a pediatric nurse. They had three children—two boys and a girl. When we first met them the youngest was about eleven years old and the oldest was fifteen or sixteen. David was the middle child. He was a slim, quiet boy who was always polite and made a point of coming into the living room to greet us whenever we visited in their home. He was friendly, but he never seemed to feel the need to draw attention to himself.

When David graduated from high school, he was at a complete loss about what he should do with his life. He said that he had spent hours in prayer, but he could not get any answers.

He knew that he wanted to do some sort of missions work, but he did not know whether he was supposed to go to college first.

A few months after his high school graduation, David got up early one morning to attend a Full Gospel Businessmen's Fellowship breakfast. During the meeting, he asked the men to pray that he would be able to find God's will for his life. He told them that he was willing to do anything that God wanted him to do, but he needed direction. The men had him sit him in a chair, laid hands on him and prayed for God's will to be revealed. God was silent.

On the way home from the meeting, a gust of wind picked up the little Volkswagen bug that he was driving and turned it upside down. David sustained severe brain injuries and was unconscious when the ambulance arrived to transport him to the hospital. He was in the hospital for a week, and during that time he celebrated his nineteenth birthday. Three days after his birthday he died without ever regaining consciousness.

During the time of David's hospitalization, John and I prayed for him constantly; hundreds of other Christians prayed for him too. Nevertheless, his life ended almost before it had begun. I could hardly accept that someone with such a heart for Jesus, someone who wanted only to serve Him, could have his life snatched from him in such a manner.

I attended the funeral alone. I was so sad and depressed that during the service I began crying. The more I tried to stop, the harder I cried. I was embarrassed because I knew that I was being disruptive, but my sobs were uncontrollable. I had no doubt that David was in Heaven, but I felt such a mournful sadness that I simply could not control myself. I cried so hard that I heard very little of what was said until the very end of the service.

In closing, the minister who officiated had all of the young people who had been saved under David's ministry stand, and then he had several of them talk about David's impact on their lives. During his last couple of years as a high school student David had started a lunch-hour Bible study at his high school. Every day during his lunch break he sat under a tree, read from his Bible and talked to anyone who was interested about the saving power of Jesus Christ. Soon he had a large crowd gathering under that tree with him, and each day he taught them from the Word of God. At his funeral those young people testified that more than three hundred fifty teens had accepted Jesus Christ as their Savior through David's lunch-hour ministry.

God had remained silent because David's ministry had ended. It had been short but powerful, and I am certain that the effects of what occurred more than thirty years ago under that tree on the grounds of that public high school are ongoing.

In the eyes of the world David had gained nothing, but in God's eyes he had run the race, crossed the finish line and achieved the crown before his nineteenth birthday!

Let He Who Lacks Wisdom Ask God

As Christian parents we hope that our children will grow up to serve God. We never consider that they might finish that service early in life, but we hope that they will live their lives in such a way that they will lead others to Christ.

I knew even before my first child was conceived that if God ever sent me children they would never truly belong to me; I believe that all children belong to God and that He allows us to be caretakers for Him. Thus, my greatest fear was that I would fail God in the awesome responsibility of raising godly children. I had no preconceived notions about what His purpose for them might be, but I believed that God did have a purpose for each of them. It was my responsibility to teach them to love and reverence Him above everything else.

As a result, long before we had our first child John and I made a commitment to bring our own lives into obedience to Jesus Christ. Although we were Christians, we did not read the Bible; therefore, we did not know exactly what living a Christian life entailed. Yet, even though we knew very little about how a Christian ought to live, we were determined to try. We soon found that whenever we sincerely sought God's will for our lives, He answered in ways that were clear and unmistakable.

In the mid 1960's John was a manager for a small loan company, and I was working as a secretary. I worked in a large bank building in downtown El Paso, and since I usually did not leave the building during my lunch break, I often picked up some yogurt at the concession stand on the first floor.

The woman who owned the stand started her business with magazines, newspapers, gum and candy, and kept expanding it until she offered numerous items, including yogurt, burritos and sandwiches. Because I saw her nearly every day, we struck up a friendship. She often mentioned that she was making more money on her concession stand than she had ever dreamed possible, and from what I could observe of her rapidly expanding business I had no reason to doubt her claims.

One day she told me that a new Holiday Inn was being built downtown about three blocks from our building. The owner had approached her about putting in a concession stand at the Holiday Inn, but she felt that she could not run both. She told me that if I wanted the Holiday Inn concession stand, she could definitely get it for me. Then she added excitedly, "You will make a lot more money there than I do here because you will sell liquor." She went on to say that there is a huge profit in selling packaged liquor. She would teach me everything I needed to know and help me get my business set up. I immediately felt uneasy about selling liquor, but I did not say anything. I told my friend that I would talk to John about it.

That evening I told John about this "business opportunity," and he was very excited. However, John agreed that selling liquor might not be what Jesus would want us to do.

The next day I told my friend that John and I would really love to have the concession, but we did not want to sell liquor. She responded that not selling liquor would be a deal breaker; it was a condition of being awarded the concession.

John and I decided to pray and ask God if selling liquor would be okay, and for the next few days we discussed the matter between the two of us constantly. This was our reasoning:

1. If people want to drink, they are going to buy liquor whether we sell it to them or not.

2. We are not going to try to persuade anyone to buy liquor; they will be coming to us.

3. Most of our sales will come from other items; everyone staying in a hotel needs toiletries, snacks, and reading material.

4. The people who buy the liquor will be taking it back to their rooms to drink it so, in a way, we will be keeping them safe by preventing them from driving drunk.

As I look back, I am embarrassed to admit that we were ever unsure of whether selling liquor was a conflict of Christian principles. Yet, although we were naïve, we were sincere. I have since discovered that when we *sincerely* seek God's will in anything, He will answer. Christians often ask God about things when they already know the answer; in such cases they do not want guidance; they want permission. In those situations, God is probably not very patient, but when we really want to know something, He is always willing to tell us.

One evening when I came home from work I pulled a piece of paper out of the mailbox. It was a tri-fold flyer from a church I had never heard of. Someone had circled a portion with a pen. It read: *"Satan never endorses God's enterprises. God's true friends never support Satan's enterprises."*

John and I were blown away! We had not told anyone about our dilemma. We had not even told anyone that we had an opportunity to be awarded the concession. The only ones who knew about our situation were John, me and God! We had received our answer. God had sent us mail!

I kept the flyer for several weeks, and from time to time I took it out and looked at it. There was no indication as to whom might have put it in our mailbox, and I was very intrigued about its origin. I was naïve, but I was pretty sure that there are no post offices in Heaven.

Finally, one day as I stood staring at the perfectly circled message, it dawned on me that since this was a tri-fold, maybe I should open it and see what was inside. When I unfolded it, I saw that it was from an acquaintance of ours who was a lay preacher in the Methodist church. He had circled his name and the time that he was going to be delivering a sermon in the church where the flyer had originated. Of course, the date of his sermon had long since passed, but the ink had bled through and made a perfect outline around God's message to John and me. I was even more amazed to discover that the ink had bled because the line was so sharp and circled those words so precisely that it was difficult to believe that this was not the message our acquaintance had meant to send.

I hope that you will remember that when you *really, sincerely* want to know something, all you have to do is ask God. He will answer—even if He has to send you mail.

The Children That God Entrusted to Me

John and I were married for seven years with no children, so, of course, when I discovered that I was pregnant, I was thrilled. I wanted to do everything right, but I was not sure what that entailed.

One Saturday evening in May of 1970 we attended our regular weekly prayer group to find that a visiting missionary was conducting the meeting. After he gave some teaching, he began to prophecy. I had never heard prophecy before, and to this day I am not certain that he was really giving prophecy, but I was very intrigued. He began by saying, "My Daughter," and he had my attention as soon as he spoke those words. I thought, "Oh, maybe this is for me." But then I immediately looked around the living room of our hosts at the five or six other women attending. I was the youngest in age and also the youngest in Christian experience. Most of them were fortyish while I was only twenty-four. Although I had been a Christian all of my life, I had been introduced to the Charismatic Movement only a few months earlier, and I knew almost nothing about the Gifts of the Spirit.

"Look at all of these women," I thought. "They are really godly women, but you are nothing." I was so busy berating myself that I heard nothing else that the visiting missionary said. I was much too busy carrying on an internal debate. "It could be for me. No it couldn't. You don't deserve to have God give you a message, and He isn't going to tell you anything...." On and on it went until I felt the missionary's hand came down on my head. At that point I stopped my silent argument and listened to what he had to say.

The only part I heard was that I was supposed to read the four Gospels straight through three times. I was to finish this task in thirty days, and when I had finished, God would tell me what I was supposed to do. Boy! Was I excited!

I had always resisted reading the Bible because I thought that it was really boring. Besides that, didn't we pay a pastor to read it for us and tell us what was in it? Reading the Bible was his job, not mine. Because of this bad attitude on my part, I had to ask one of the women at the group, "What are the four Gospels?"

She answered, "Matthew, Mark, Luke and John."

I was relieved. That didn't sound too bad; I was pretty sure that I could do that. Thus, I began reading feverishly. I wanted to make certain that I finished all four Gospels three times before the thirty days ended. I was pretty sure that if I did, something stupendous would happen. I thought that probably an angel would visit me and give me a message that would change the world, or commission me to go to some faraway place and perform miracles in the name of Jesus.

I counted off the days like a child waiting for Christmas. Just before the time ended I went out and bought snacks just in case the angel might be hungry or just in case I might receive a visit from a human who was going to bring me God's message—humans are always hungry. When the final day arrived, I was ready. I had managed to finish all of the reading and the snacks were in the fridge. The day passed, and no one came. I was disappointed, but I thought that maybe God wanted John to be there when the messenger arrived and that he would probably come that evening. When John got home from work, I served dinner and warned him not to eat the snacks.

We waited all evening. I was six months pregnant with my first child, and I was tired. Finally, we determined that no one was coming, and there was nothing else for us to do but go to bed.

The next day I prayed and asked God what I was supposed to do. It was one of the few times in my life that I have heard clearly and unmistakably from God. He answered, "Keep reading." I have never been more surprised! Those thirty days of Bible reading had been designed to get me into the habit of reading the Bible. I was so stubborn that I had to be tricked into a daily Bible reading! I learned right then and there that we are not the ones who make the rules concerning what we need to do to serve God.

I have read the Bible every day since, and because I was pregnant, I read it out loud so that my unborn baby could hear it too. I took the Bible to the hospital when Alexandra was born, and I read it to her the first time the nurse brought her to me. She was always part of my Bible reading, and as other children came along, they were also part of our daily Bible reading routine.

After we began our homeschool, it worked out best to have our Bible reading early in the morning. While the children ate breakfast, I read aloud to them from the Bible, two chapters from the Old Testament and two chapters from the New Testament. I kept a bookmark in each testament and read straight through. After we finished our Bible reading, we joined hands around the table and prayed aloud with each person praying in turn. This is a wonderful way to begin the day, and I encourage all families to adopt this custom.

Every time we finished, we started all over again. After a while I stopped keeping track of the number of times we had gone through the Bible, but I do know that by the time

Alexandra was twelve, she had heard the Bible twenty times. Of course, each of the children, from the oldest to the youngest baby, was required to be present for these daily Bible readings; therefore, the determining factor in how many times they had heard the Bible was their ages.

What Would Jesus Do?

Regardless of how diligently you work to instill Christian values in your children, if you do not provide a good example for them with your own life, you will not succeed. Never require anything of them that you do not require of yourself.

Jesus came to earth for several reasons. Primarily, He came to give himself as a sacrifice for our sins. If He had not done that, we would be without hope. However, He also came to show us how to live. Jesus lived a perfect life to provide an example for us. If we had nothing of the Bible except the four Gospels, we would know exactly how we are supposed to conduct ourselves in every aspect of our lives. We would know how to treat other people; we would know what our relationship to God is supposed to be; we would know how to deal with our enemies and how to treat our parents. There is no aspect of the human experience that is not covered in those Gospels.

In recent years the WWJD bracelets have become popular. It is a simple concept—in every situation ask yourself,

"What would Jesus do?" I wish that more of the people wearing those bracelets would live out that sentiment. If we would actually stop to ask ourselves what Jesus would do in every situation, most of us would live our lives very differently. Of course, to ask that question with any hope of being able to determine what Jesus would do in a particular situation requires that we know what Jesus did do when He was here in human form.

I believe that a big part of the problem with Christians living in a manner that is totally inconsistent with genuine Christianity is that most of them don't have a clue when it comes to WWJD. We rely on other people's interpretations of what Jesus would do based on their personal expectations of what they would like to think He would do. Christians tend to put God/Jesus into one of several categories:

- The wimpy Jesus who doesn't want to upset anyone and just wants us all to get along and be nice.
- The pompous Jesus who sits in Heaven and looks down on us and laughs because we are so ridiculous in the way we play out the human experience.
- The vengeful Jesus clinching a fistful of lightning bolts that He is preparing to unleash to pay us back for all the bad things we have done.

- The distant Jesus who is watching us from a bazillion miles away and can only see us as teeny-tiny specks and is really not interested in us as individuals.

Although each of these ideas of what Jesus is like has gained a certain amount of acceptance among Christians, none of them gives us an accurate picture of Jesus. We will never begin to understand who Jesus is until we get to know Him through the scriptures, and we will never get to know Him until we immerse ourselves in His Word.

Have you ever thought about why God created families? Why is the parent such an important part of a child's life? I have a theory that God gave us parents because they are the first example of God/Jesus that we encounter. We have all heard stories about people with abusive fathers or negligent mothers who had a difficult time becoming Christians because they could not relate to God as their parent. The last thing they wanted in their lives was another disappointing parent.

The Christian man who was the most instrumental person in helping John and me to fully commit our lives to Christ told us a very interesting story about his own experience in coming to Christ. Ed was an only child, and when he was a little boy his mother left his father and him. He spent his whole life mourning because his mother had deserted him and wondering what had prompted her to do it.

Even after Ed was grown, he still felt so unloved that he was unable to move past the hurt of having been deserted by his mother. One day when he was reading the Bible, he came across Isaiah 49 and read these words: *"Can a mother forget her little child and not have love for her own son? Yet, even if that should be, I will not forget you."* (TLB) Ed said that the pain and sadness that had always been a part of his life just melted away and he knew that God was not only a father to him but a mother as well. From that moment he began to feel loved, and he began to heal.

Yes, God is the perfect parent who never deserts us and never stops loving us, but before we meet Him, we meet our earthly parents. For those of us who are parents it is imperative that we provide a good example for our children. They meet us long before they meet Jesus, and their initial opinion of Him is going to depend to a great extent on their opinion of us.

Your children are always watching you. If they see that you are only giving lip service to the rules you have established for them, they will not feel obligated to adhere to them either. You may bully them into more or less complying when you are present, but the moment your back is turned, they will do whatever they like because they will know that you do not really believe what you are telling them.

I never asked my children to do anything I was not willing to do myself. When we added scripture memorization to our spiritual training, I learned the same scriptures they did. Each week we chose a scripture to memorize. We took turns with a different family member choosing the scripture each week. The scriptures were always fairly long and took some effort to memorize. At the end of the week, I quizzed each child. If they were not able to recite the week's scripture word perfect, they had to go back and study some more until they could recite it satisfactorily. I did give them a break so that from Thursday until Sunday any time that they were ready to recite their scripture, they could let me know and I would quiz them. If they recited it correctly, they were through for the week. Consequently, they usually completed their recitations on Thursday. I usually did my recitation on Thursday, too. I would hand the Bible to one of the older children and recite for them. If I were not word perfect, I had to go back and study some more and then be quizzed again.

I always adhered to the same television viewing rules that I had for them. We had very strict guidelines in terms of sexual content, language, and violence, and I never watched anything that I considered unacceptable for them. My youngest child moved out in 2003, and I still live my life by those rules that I set for them so many years ago.

Remember, sin is not determined by the age of the sinner. People talk about what is and is not appropriate for children. While there are certainly some subjects that might be disturbing to a child, such as a documentary dealing with the atrocities committed during the Holocaust, that might be appropriate and even beneficial for adults to explore, most things that are not appropriate for children are not appropriate for anyone.

A simple test is to ask yourself why you object to your child being exposed to a particular movie or book or activity. If your objections are due to moral content, then that particular activity is not appropriate for you either. If you ignore this obvious conclusion you are sending a message to your children that says, "It's okay to do anything you want after you reach age twenty-one."

If you want your children to live lives that honor Christ, you must commit your own life completely and without reservation.

In 1985 John lost his job of seventeen years. He was making a six-figure income, and we had never had to worry about money. We had always lived modestly, but suddenly, without warning, everything was gone. For the next thirteen years we were destitute.

Having no income was scary enough, but I had ten children between the ages of fourteen years and two years, and I did not know how we were going to feed or clothe them. We had some savings and John's retirement, but I knew that would not last very long.

As I had come to know Christ better, I had tried to always live my life to honor Him. I made plenty of mistakes, but if I believed that He wanted me to do something, I did it—no matter how difficult. I could hardly accept that He had deserted us. I was not angry with God, but I was very sad. When I went to bed at night, I turned onto my side and cried silently. I decided that God must hate me. I know that belief stemmed partially from the fact that my own father deserted our family when I was only eight years old, and I never saw or heard from him again. I became convinced that there was something about me that was so unlovable that no one—not even God—could love me. I had tried hard to be a good daughter to Him, and He had taken everything from us and turned his back.

One night as I lay crying myself to sleep I decided that I could not go on this way. I told God that I loved him and I was going to serve him, no matter what. I said, "You are God, and you have every right to hate me because you are righteous, but I am never going to leave you. I have spent fifteen years doing everything that I believed you wanted me to do, and I can't turn back now. If you want to get rid of me, you are going to have to kill me."

Afterwards, I felt calmer than I had in a long while. I would like to tell you that everything immediately improved, but that is not what happened. I was only three months into the thirteen years, and the really rough times were still ahead of us.

Nevertheless, I had settled in my own mind that my relationship with Jesus Christ is not about me; it is about Him. He is worthy to be worshiped; He is worthy to be praised; He is God.

Every Christian must come to this point at some time in her Christian walk. I hope that you will not have to go through anything as devastating as I did, but you must come to that moment in your own life when you define your relationship with Jesus Christ. In doing so you must conclude that it's not about you; it's about Him.

That is what Jesus would do. Oh, yes, that is what He did do on the cross when He surrendered His will to the Father's will and gave himself as a living sacrifice for our sins.

In I Corinthians 10 Paul writes, "I try to please everyone in everything I do, not doing what I like or what is best for me, but what is best for them, so that they may be saved."

If we want our children to live the kind of disciplined lives that will not only make them a blessing to us and to society but will bring them into obedience to God and result in their salvation, we must be willing to provide an example in our own lives that will point the way to that salvation. That is what training a child in the way he should go is all about.

Money Can't Buy Happiness, but It Does Pay the Rent

Will Rogers once told a story about a rancher who was going through some difficult financial times: One day as the rancher stood gazing at his field of horses, he decided that if he could train them to get by without eating he could save a good deal of money. Each day he fed the animals a little less than the previous day until he finally reached a point where he was able to stop feeding them altogether. The rancher was elated! Surely this was the best money-saving idea he had ever had!

A week later the rancher drove his truck out to the field to check on his horses and found that every one of them was dead. "Oh! No!" he exclaimed, "Just when they had learned to live without eating, they all had to go and die on me!"

We, too, were experiencing severe financial difficulties, but training ten children to live without eating was out of the question. We had to find ways to make every penny stretch—just to meet our basic expenses. In addition, we had all of our school expenses. Every day was a challenge.

When the children were earning their undergraduate degrees from BYU, they completed all course work at home, but they were required to take a two-week on-campus seminar for each of the five areas of study and a one-week closure seminar. That was a total of eleven weeks of on-campus seminars for each child. If we were to stay on schedule, it was imperative that each of our BYU students take at least some seminars every summer.

Paying for the basic courses was almost impossible, but adding to that the cost of taking the children to the campus where we had additional housing and meal expenses along with the additional costs of seminars presented a nearly insurmountable obstacle. As the older children graduated, they began working and contributing financially, but even with huge sacrifices on their parts, we could barely make ends meet.

The seminars took place only once a year during the summer months so that people could take their vacations to attend. Therefore, if a student missed a particular seminar, he could not make it up for an entire year.

One summer I needed to send three of the children to the campus to take seminars. In order to do that, I needed five thousand dollars. I prayed and prayed, but no financial solution was in sight. There did not seem to be any way that we could get the five thousand dollars, but I went ahead and made the seminar arrangements. I reserved the children's places in their seminar classes (the money could be paid in one lump sum on the first day of the seminar). I got their clothes ready. I made the reservations for an on-campus apartment. The only thing I lacked was the five thousand dollars.

As we approached the final two weeks before the seminar began, I was becoming desperate. My prayers had turned into spiritual begging. *"Pleeeease God! Pleeeease send us five thousand dollars. You know that I am only homeschooling because you told me to do this. I haaaave to have this money. I don't know what to do. Pleeeease, pleeeease, pleeeease, help me!"*

During this time, when John was reading the newspaper one day, he came across an advertisement posted by someone who wanted to buy mortgages at a reduced rate.

In 1979 we had sold five acres of land in El Paso's lower valley, and we had provided owner financing. The remaining balance of the mortgage was only ten thousand dollars, but if we could sell the mortgage to the person who had placed the ad, it would probably give us enough money to send the children to BYU for their seminars.

John talked very straight to me. He explained that when anyone "buys paper" they do so at a greatly reduced price. Since about fifty percent of the balance of the note is pretty standard, we would be very fortunate if we got the entire five thousand dollars.

I was ecstatic! I had asked God for five thousand dollars, and it looked as if He were going to give it to me.

John set up an appointment, and since we held the mortgage on the land jointly, we went together to the office of the potential buyer. The address in downtown El Paso turned out to be the shop of an elderly Jewish pawnbroker. He was extremely courteous, but it was immediately apparent that he was a tough businessman. I braced myself for a hard bargain.

John and I sat down opposite him and handed him the documents; neither of us said a word. The old man read them and then looked up at us over the top of his bifocals. "I'll give you nine thousand dollars," he said.

For a moment I thought that I had not heard him correctly. I sat staring stupidly but silently while John told him that we accepted his offer.

The old pawnbroker had us sign some paperwork and told us to take everything to his attorney whose offices were about three blocks away. He instructed us to then return to his pawn shop and pick up our check. In less than thirty minutes we had our five thousand dollars for the seminars and four thousand additional dollars for our family to live on for the next two months.

They're Rare—That's Why They Call Them Miracles

God always provided for us, but we rarely saw miracles. For the most part, we had to do the things necessary to make certain that our children were fed and clothed. Fortunately, we had purchased a house with a low payment—our escrowed mortgage payment was less than six hundred dollars a month. We were, therefore, able to stay in our house in the country.

We had never eaten out very often. John and I had been accustomed to having dinner out alone together on Friday evenings, and we took the children to a cafeteria every Sunday after church. Otherwise, we ate at home with the girls and me doing the cooking. After John lost his job, however, there was no eating out for any reason. Besides that, I had to learn to prepare meals really cheaply.

I discovered that I could purchase ten-pound bags of chicken quarters for thirty-nine cents a pound. Consequently, we ate chicken every day for several years. I learned how to cook chicken in every way imaginable: fried chicken, baked chicken, chicken tacos, chicken enchiladas, hot chicken salad, etc., etc., etc. Fortunately, I am a good cook so our meals were actually quite tasty, but after a while we all grew really tired of chicken.

I had always handed clothes down to the younger children and exercised restraint in making new clothing purchases, but now this practice had to be taken to the extreme.

Winter "at home" clothes consisted of one pair of tennis shoes, three pairs of jeans and three sweatshirts for each child. The summer wardrobe was one pair of tennis shoes, three tee shirts, and any combination of three pairs of shorts and/or jeans for each child. Some of the boys refused to wear shorts and others liked them, so I left that jeans/shorts decision up to each individual child.

Our towels and sheets became threadbare, and our house badly needed repairs, but we had a roof over our heads and food on the table, and our homeschool was always in session. We learned to be content with our lives and grateful that God always supplied our needs.

He Knows Our Needs Before We Pray

A popular Christian song says, "He knows our needs before we pray, And we can rest assured the answer's on the way." I was frequently amazed to see how time after time God looked ahead, saw our needs well in advance, and made provision to help us through some tough times.

After *No Regrets* was published Alexandra and I both accepted as many invitations to speak as possible, and the money we received as speakers was an important source of income for our family. Our expenses were paid, and we received an honorarium. In addition, we sold our tapes and books at these events.

In the spring of 1991 Alexandra spoke to a group of homeschoolers, and on the return trip her plane was delayed for several hours. When all the passengers were boarded and the plane was finally ready to take off, the stewardess announced that to make up for the delay the airlines would be giving one lucky passenger a free round-trip ticket to anywhere in the United States. She then announced the seat number of the winner.

Alexandra did not even bother to check her seat number. The stewardess kept calling for the winner to identify himself, and finally the man sitting next to Alexandra said, "It's you. You're the winner."

I was thrilled for her. She had given up so much for her family. Everything she had she gave to the family, and I felt that this was God's way of doing something special for her. I asked her where she wanted to go with her free ticket. She told me that she did not have anywhere that she wanted to go.

The ticket was good for only one year, and as the months passed, I began to exert some pressure on her to use it. I kept saying that she needed to treat herself to a vacation with that free ticket. She was working as a history instructor at the El Paso Community College and would have been doing well if she had not given every penny she earned to the family. She could use some of her own money to have a nice vacation with that free ticket.

In February, 1992, when my mother was seventy years old, she was diagnosed with cancer. She had surgery and afterwards had to undergo chemotherapy. I really wanted to visit her, but I knew that was impossible so I talked to her on the phone and prayed for her with great fervor. I never said anything to my family about wanting to make the trip to see her because it was simply out of the question.

One day Alexandra came to me and said that she was certain that God had given her that free airline ticket so that I could fly to Kansas to see my mother. I adamantly refused. She insisted. Finally she told me that she had checked the expiration date on the ticket and that it would expire in one week.

I quickly made my reservations and was able to spend three days with my mother right after she came home from the hospital. My stepfather was with her, and she now had plenty of money. I did not really *need* to be with her, but God knew that I *should* be with her, and He provided a way for that to happen a whole year in advance.

I made a 1400 mile round trip with only ten dollars in my purse. I took my best "at home" slacks, a pair of old Dockers with an iron-on patch on the knee, and an old dress that still looked pretty good. My stepfather had his birthday while I was there, and I did not know what to do for a gift. I finally went to Braums and bought two ice-cream sundaes to go, one for my mother and one for him, and I wished him a happy birthday.

When my mother asked me why I only bought two I said, "I didn't want one. I'm on a diet." Ten dollars wasn't much, but it was enough to do what I needed to do.

The day I flew home was the expiration date for the ticket. God has great timing!

One of the most important lessons that I learned during those thirteen years is that what we want and what we need are rarely the same things. God did not always give us everything we wanted, but He always gave us everything we needed. Sometimes what we needed was to not get what we wanted.

Who Is God?

The Bible is filled with names for God that describe various aspects of His character. He is:

El Shaddai—the all sufficient one

Jehovah-Jireh—the Lord who provides

Jehovah-Rophe—the Lord who heals

Jehovah-Shammah—the Lord who is there

Immanuel—the God who is with us

I do not regret any of the difficulties that I personally endured because through each of them I was able to experience God in a way that I might never have under better circumstances.

It is a sad truth that most of us do not experience God until we have a need in our own lives.

If John had not lost his job and we had not gone through those thirteen agonizing years, I might never have known God as *El Shaddai*, the all-sufficient one. When everything was gone, I had to recognize that He and He alone is sufficient to meet all our needs. I discovered that whether those needs are physical, spiritual, or emotional, He is always the all-sufficient one.

Desperate circumstances brought me face to face with *Jehovah-Jireh*, the Lord who provides. Whether I needed the money to pay school expenses or a plane ticket to see my sick mother, He worked miracles on my behalf. If money had not been a consideration, I would have sent the tuition to the school and bought the plane ticket without ever considering that everything that we have comes from the hand of the Lord who provides. Thus, I would never have experienced the joy of knowing that Jesus Christ not only sees my present circumstances, He looks ahead and makes provision years in advance for the day when those needs will occur.

If Israel had not suffered the intussusception and I had not been run over by my own van, I might never have met *Jehovah-Rophe*, the Lord who heals. I have never doubted that only the healing power of the Lord Jesus Christ kept us both alive and returned us to perfect health.

When John lost his job, we were cut off from nearly everyone we knew. People we thought were our friends quickly distanced themselves from us. One day we were sought after; the next we were avoided. That is when I met *Jehovah-Shammah*, the Lord who is there. He never deserts us, is never embarrassed by us, and never looks the other way. He is *Immanuel,* the God who is with us, always and forever.

It's 2010—Do You Know Where Your Children Are?

It has now been ten years since our youngest finished school. Those little children whom I believed would always be my babies are now grown men and women with families and careers. They have been through some personal trials and tribulations of their own, but I continue to hold them up in prayer daily, and I trust that God will help each of them to become the people He created them to be and to finish the work He has for them.

Alexandra

When Alexandra was eighteen years old, she began teaching History at the El Paso Community College. She knew from the beginning that this was not where she wanted to spend the rest of her working life, but she also knew that she needed to get some experience before she could be taken seriously in the business world.

After four years of teaching, Alexandra resigned her position and began looking for that special niche where she would fit in. She went to work for a large corporation and did extremely well. She was in sales and was one of the company's top producers in this area.

After she had been with the company for a year or so they sent her to Dallas to attend a three-day training seminar. During that seminar, the trainer made the statement that there are two kinds of people—corporate people and small business people. Nobody is both, so it is important to discover which type you are. That was a defining moment in Alexandra's life because she realized that she was definitely not a corporate person.

As a result, in 1998, at the age of twenty-seven, Alexandra cashed in a small IRA and, with only eleven thousand dollars, opened Frontier 2000 Mortgage. She discovered that she loved being a small business person. I have heard her say many times that her worst day as a self-employed businesswoman was better than her best day in the corporate world.

She has worked hard and has been very successful with the mortgage company. In the spring of 2003 Frontier 2000 Mortgage was able to purchase its own office building complete with an attached warehouse and private parking lot.

Alexandra has also continued to be active in her community. She has served as the President of the Women's Council of Builders and the President of the El Paso Association of Mortgage Brokers. She currently serves on the board of the El Paso Hispanic Chamber of Commerce. When the committee extended the invitation to accept a board position, she pointed out to them that she is not Hispanic. They told her that they already knew that; they were looking for a successful businesswoman to fill the position. Alexandra has been a board member since 2005, and in December of 2010 she became the Chairperson.

Alexandra has received numerous awards in recognition of her work, but it is her honesty and integrity that set her apart. She is generous with her time, her money, and her talents. She never sees her competitors as threats; she believes that everyone in the business community should do everything they can to help others succeed, and she puts those sentiments into practice by encouraging her competitors and helping them solve problems they cannot solve alone. Alexandra is a genuine example of a modern Christian woman who is in this world but not of this world.

Christopher

Christopher had a hard time finding something to kick start his career. He did not want to teach so, after quite a bit of searching, he took a job at the local racetrack as a photographer. It was his job to video all of the races so that the track would have a video record of each. He had never used a camera before, but he did a really good job.

After about a year he felt that he had enough experience to apply for a job as a photographer at the local television stations. He did not know that these jobs normally go to people with extensive experience shooting news footage and that there is a considerable amount of competition for every opening.

One day as his shift was ending at the track he received a call from the CBS affiliate in El Paso, and they asked him to come over immediately. When he arrived at the station, the news director told him that he was going to give him an "audition." If he were able to satisfactorily complete the assignment, he was hired. The news director handed him a television camera, which was a great deal more sophisticated than the one he used at the track, and told him that a new general had arrived at Ft. Bliss and that the ceremony to change command would take place in one hour. He then told Christopher to go to Ft. Bliss, shoot the ceremony, and bring the footage back to the station in time for the six o'clock news. It was already late afternoon so the pressure was on.

Christopher called me and blurted out the story. He said that he was on his way to Ft. Bliss and that I should pray for him and watch the news at six to see his footage. When he told me that they were sending him alone, I was really concerned for him. If he were unable to come back with the footage, the story would not make the news and he would not get the job.

Christopher did arrive on time, shoot the footage, and get it back to the station in time for the six o'clock news. As a result, he was hired on the spot. At the time, none of us knew anything about television news so we did not truly appreciate how unusual a circumstance this was.

A few weeks after he was hired, someone at the station told Christopher the rest of the story: The news director had gotten into a huge argument with one of the photographers, and the photographer had threatened to quit and leave the station in a bind. The news director shouted that he could replace the photographer with anyone and that his replacement would be able to do an equally good job. To prove his point, he opened the file cabinet, reached in without looking, and pulled out the first employment application that he touched. The news director then told the photographer that he was going to call whoever had filled out that application and hire him as the photographer's replacement.

If it had not been for the news director's determination to prove to his photographer that he was not indispensible, Christopher would never have been considered because there were actually a number of applications from "qualified" applicants in that file cabinet. God has His ways of using situations to open doors for His children that would, otherwise, forever remain closed. I can just imagine that on the day when Christopher took the job at the racetrack God was saying, "Don't worry. It's not for long."

A year later Christopher went to work for the ABC affiliate in El Paso, and he has now been there for twenty years. He is the operations manager for the station and also owns his own media production company. Through his production company he has done work for "Good Morning America" and he worked on the movie "The Day After Tomorrow." He has also done work for ESPN and has worked on a number of national commercials. Currently he has the contract to do the training videos for Texas Workforce Commission.

In 2008 Christopher married the woman who is the news director for the ABC affiliate here in El Paso. He was thirty-six years old, and it was a first marriage for both of them.

Francesca

At age seventeen Francesca began teaching history at the El Paso Community College. She was very fortunate in that Alexandra was already working there, and that helped her get her teaching job at such a young age. She loved teaching and never had any real interest in doing anything else.

At age twenty-one Francesca married. She taught for several years but before long began a family. She has two girls and one boy ranging in age from fifteen years to twelve years.

Francesca and her family now live in Phoenix where she homeschools her children.

Dominic

Christopher helped Dominic break into news photography right after he finished school. As a result, Dominic began working as a television news photographer in El Paso when he was barely seventeen years old. A few years later he took a job in Kansas City, but the work was generally safe, so I was happy for him and felt that I had little to worry about.

In 2004 when Dominic went to work as a photographer for CNN, all that changed. His job has allowed him to travel to many parts of the world; that is the upside. Most of the time he is sent to locations where there is either a shooting war or a particularly dangerous natural disaster; that is the downside.

Dominic was sent to New Orleans just before Katrina hit so that he would be on site to shoot footage of the devastation that everyone knew was sure to come. He was sent to Haiti immediately following the earthquake, and the horror stories he told when he visited us afterwards still give me chills. He has been to Iraq three times, and he has been to Afghanistan twice.

Dominic has experienced the aftermaths of a number of serious earthquakes in various parts of the world. He has been pelted with rain from hurricanes driven by winds so strong that he could barely stay on his feet. He has gone without food and water for twenty-four hours at a time because everything was contaminated. He has been shot at when he was embedded with the troops in the Middle East.

Dominic is an excellent photographer and has done some exceptional work. While he was in Iraq he put together a documentary titled *Combat Hospital* that aired on CNN December of 2007. Dominic filmed, edited, produced and directed it. *Combat Hospital* was his tribute to the American military doctors in Iraq whose work he admired so much.

Early on I had to learn to pray for Dominic and then trust him to God's protection. I remind myself that every day people die in car crashes, in household accidents, and from all sorts of diseases. There is no place of safety apart from Jesus Christ. This is the work that Dominic has chosen, and I have learned to trust that God will protect him.

Victoria

When Victoria was eight years old, she began praying every day for a husband. She took a lot of teasing from her siblings who thought that it was ridiculous to pray for a husband at age eight. Victoria, however, was not to be discouraged. She dreamed of the day when the Lord would send her a handsome Christian husband who would love her and take care of her.

Victoria was so determined that she was going to live a storybook life that even as an eight year old she left no stone unturned. One day she told me that she had found a frog in our yard and had kissed him to see if he would turn into a prince. When I asked her what she would have done if he had turned into a prince, she responded, "I would have kissed him again and turned him back into a frog."

Victoria was also determined that she and her husband would have two beautiful children—one boy and one girl—and the four of them would live happily ever after. I do not know whether she prayed for the boy and girl when she was a child, but they were definitely part of her plan. As she grew older, she never lowered her expectations. One day when she was in her late teens I suggested that she might have two boys or two girls since it is impossible to predetermine the sex of an unborn child. She just stared at me as if I did not understand. She answered me as patiently as if I were a confused child, "No, I want one boy and one girl."

It actually became a sort of inside joke among our family members that Victoria was either unwilling or unable accept the possibility that she might not get exactly what she wanted. Since she was always incredibly sweet and totally obedient, the whole family humored her. We just went along with her notion that someday her prince would come along and she would have two beautiful, adorable children—one boy and one girl—and they would all live happily ever after.

When Victoria was twenty years old, we were attending a small Baptist church in the tiny town of Canutillo about three miles from our house. One day a young man twenty-one years of age decided that he would drive the twenty-five miles from his home on the East side of El Paso to visit our church. Our pastor had been his youth pastor when he was in his early teens, and he had not seen him for years. That morning, however, Jeremy decided that he wanted to visit his former youth pastor's church.

Victoria was not in church that day because she had been scheduled to work a morning shift, but when John and I saw Jeremy, we both felt that he would be perfect for Victoria. Since he was only visiting, however, we knew that she was probably not going to have the chance to meet him.

To our surprise, the following Sunday Jeremy returned and Victoria was there. When they saw each other, it was love at first sight. They met the first week in October and were married on December 23. Under almost any other circumstances both John and I and Jeremy's parents would have objected to such a brief courtship, but we all knew that God had put them together.

Two and a half weeks after their first date, he bought her an engagement ring and came to our house to ask John and me for our blessing before he proposed. He told us, "I may not always be able to give Victoria everything she wants, but I will always work hard and try to give her everything she wants."

Their wedding was made even more beautiful by all of the Christmas decorations with dozens of tiny white lights and several hundred candles. To add to the fairytale atmosphere, when our pastor pronounced them man and wife, the bride and groom shared their first kiss. It was Victoria's first kiss ever.

Victoria and Jeremy just celebrated their fourteenth wedding anniversary. They have two beautiful, adorable children—one boy and one girl—and are living happily ever after in Dallas.

Benjamin

When Benjamin was ten years old, he said that when he grew up he wanted to be "just like Peter Jennings." This was before his brothers were working in television news so his desire to become a news anchor was not based on anything that he was seeing up close and personal.

Benjamin also had a second love; he was always drawn to the ministry. In fact, he impressed our Baptist church in Canutillo sufficiently that the pastor asked him to become the youth pastor when he was only sixteen years old. Benjamin accepted the position and, among other things, brought to the church the *True Love Waits* program which encourages young people to pledge to remain abstinent until they marry. He was the youth pastor for about two years and during that time, he had an opportunity to deliver several sermons to the entire congregation. He was hooked!

Although Benjamin has never attended seminary, the Lord has worked in "mysterious ways" to help him combine his love for television news and his love for ministry. When he was twenty years old, Benjamin applied for a position as an assistant pastor at a very old Presbyterian Church in Portland, Oregon. After a number of telephone interviews with various board members and at least one conference call, the church asked him to come to Portland to spend a weekend and "audition" for the position.

By this time Benjamin was working as a news photographer and was engaged. He and Jasmine were planning their wedding for the spring of 2000. The committee, therefore, decided that they wanted to meet Jasmine too. They paid for both of them to make the trip from El Paso to Portland and furnished accommodations for each of them for the weekend.

Benjamin called me the day that they were ready to come home and said that he had gotten the job. He was elated, but he was a little hesitant to move so far away from his family to a place where he did not know anyone.

Later that day Benjamin called again to tell me that he and Jasmine were stranded in the Portland airport because of a problem with the plane. After a ten-hour delay, the passengers received word that the airline might put them on a flight that would go through Las Vegas, but it would get in so late that they could not get another flight out of Vegas until the next morning. He called again to ask me whether—if they did end up going through Las Vegas and having an eight-hour layover—it would be okay for Jasmine and him to get married. He said that he wouldn't if it were going to upset me, but they thought that maybe they should just go ahead and get married so that Jasmine could go to Portland with him. Thus, on June 21, 1999, (my birthday) Benjamin and Jasmine were married in a Las Vegas wedding chapel.

After a year in Portland it became apparent to Benjamin that the church was much too liberal for him and apparent to the church that Benjamin was much too conservative for them. While a number of the congregants did hold conservative Christian values, the majority supported a liberal agenda that embraced many practices that are not consistent with true Christianity. He resigned and returned to El Paso.

Benjamin quickly landed a job as the assistant pastor at a large downtown Methodist church. He also immediately went back to work as a news photographer, but he was determined that he was going to have a career in front of the camera, not behind it. "Everyone," including his broadcast news savvy brothers, told him that no one makes the jump from photographer to the anchor desk, but Benjamin was undaunted.

In 2001 the opportunity arose for Benjamin to make that "impossible" move. The Fox Television affiliate where he worked wanted to open a bureau in Las Cruces to cover all of the Las Cruces and Southern New Mexico news. Since it was going to be a one-man bureau, they wanted someone who could be both the photographer and the reporter. Benjamin seized the opportunity, packed up his wife and baby—the first of five children—and moved the twenty-five miles from El Paso, Texas, to Las Cruces, New Mexico. It was a small beginning, but it was a beginning.

Benjamin loved reporting just as much as he had believed that he would. He was soon digging into stories and reporting them with a flair not often seen on local news broadcasts. While most of the stories were not very important in terms of making a lasting impact, soon an event occurred that allowed Benjamin to combine his zeal and his talent to help change New Mexico law.

On July 19, 2002, Brianna Lopez, a five-month old girl, was taken to the emergency room of a Las Cruces, New Mexico hospital where she died shortly after her arrival. A medical examination revealed that she had been bitten repeatedly and had experienced extreme head trauma. In addition, she had been raped.

The police determined that the twenty-one bite marks were from Brianna's nineteen-year-old mother, and the head trauma and rape occurred during a "game" that her twenty-one-year-old father and her mother's nineteen-year-old twin brother had played with her. The two men took turns throwing the baby into the air so that she hit the ceiling of their mobile home and then fell to the floor. This apparently went on for hours with them taking turns raping her at intervals.

Benjamin's own two-year-old daughter was named Brianna, and I think that gave him a special concern for the tiny victim. At any rate, he devoted a huge amount of his time to reporting on the Baby Brianna murder. When the facts of the case became public, the community was outraged, but at that time New Mexico law allowed a maximum prison sentence of only eighteen years for child abuse resulting in death. With time off for good behavior, most people served only nine years for murdering their children. The citizens were appalled by the knowledge that those who were responsible for torturing and murdering Baby Brianna would receive only a slap on the wrist.

Benjamin interviewed Susanna Martinez, the District Attorney, and devoted considerable coverage to her efforts to have the law changed. He even accompanied a charter bus full of Las Cruces residents to the state capitol in Santa Fe to petition to have the law changed. He reported on the entire trip, providing nightly news coverage of the events taking place in Santa Fe, and he included his interviews with Governor Bill Richardson concerning the Baby Brianna case.

On March 31, 2005, Governor Richardson arrived in Las Cruces to sign Senate Bill 166 into law. That law, known as "The Baby Brianna Law," makes child abuse resulting in death a crime that carries a life sentence in New Mexico.

By this time Benjamin had moved back to El Paso and was anchoring the nightly news, but following the signing, Governor Richardson sent him a plaque bearing the pen that he used to sign the bill into law. The inscription on the plaque reads, "Ben, thank you for your continual efforts on behalf of Brianna to see this bill become law." It is signed, "Bill Richardson, Governor of New Mexico."

The entire time that Benjamin was working in Las Cruces he kept his job as the assistant at the church in El Paso, and within a few years he became the "Lead Teacher" and delivered the sermon for the eleven o'clock Sunday service. Because he did not attend seminary, the church had a difficult time giving him a title that did not violate their rules concerning pastors. However, God has always worked it out so that Benjamin has been able to preach.

In 2008, Benjamin was hired to anchor the five o'clock, six o'clock and ten o'clock nightly news for the NBC affiliate in El Paso, and in his "free time" he did quite a lot of work for the Christian television station here. One Sunday evening in November of 2010, Benjamin and his family stopped by the house to tell us that he was taking a job as the main anchor for the Fox affiliate in Cincinnati, Ohio. He had also found a church in Ohio where he could pursue lay ministry. We said goodbye to his family the Saturday after Thanksgiving, and we pray that God will continue to use him in Ohio. God has honored Benjamin's desire to "bring the truth" to as many people as possible whether it is through sermons delivered from the pulpit or through hard-hitting news stories that raise public awareness of issues that need to be addressed.

Israel

By the time Israel was in his early teens, it was apparent that he was a very talented artist. He began by drawing cartoon characters—usually Donald Duck and his nephews Huey, Dewey, and Louie. However, he soon abandoned the practice of copying other people's work and began creating beautiful original pieces. He primarily drew women's faces. None of the faces was that of a real woman, but each of them was gorgeous.

One particularly beautiful face was that of a young woman who appeared to be in her early to mid-twenties. It was a pencil drawing, but even though it was black and white, she was undoubtedly blonde. The only color in the picture was her eyes, which were emerald green. The moment I saw it I knew that if Alexandra and I ever had an opportunity to publish *The Twelfth Juror*, a novel that we had co-written two years earlier, I wanted to use that image for our book cover.

When Israel was seventeen, he began working as a news photographer, and even in the world of news photography, his artistry shone through. For instance, he was able to create a good deal of interest in a story about a fifteen-year-old girl who was killed by a teenage driver who was drag racing on a Saturday afternoon. He persuaded the news director of the ABC affiliate where he worked in El Paso to allow him to interview the girl's aunt without a reporter being present. The only audio on the news story was the aunt talking about her love for her niece whom she had raised from infancy. The photography was exquisite. The close-ups showed only the aunt's eyes and her profile with tears streaming down her face as she talked. The piece was so moving that the station devoted more than three minutes to this interview when it aired during the six p.m. news broadcast. It is the only time I can remember crying while watching the news.

When he was twenty-three, Israel won both first and second place in the General Assignments category from the Texas Associated Press Broadcasters. I have been told, although I have never been able to confirm this next part, that this is the first time anyone had ever won both first and second place in the same category in the same year.

Before the winners were even announced, however, Israel had decided that he was tired of news photography. He resigned and went to work for his brother Christopher who was producing a real estate program in Los Angeles through his media production company. Israel stayed there several years until the real estate market crashed.

In April of 2008 I received a call from Israel saying that he was at the hospital. He had begun experiencing excruciating abdominal pain and had gone to the emergency room. Tests revealed that a staple that had been used in his surgery when he was a baby had broken and made a small tear in his intestine. They had to do surgery.

Once again we began praying that God would intervene. After his surgery Israel was horribly sick. Instead of returning to normal, his intestine shut down completely. The doctor said that it was as if it were "cemented" together. He told Israel that he was going to have to remove the damaged portion and do a colostomy. Since so much of his intestine needed to be removed, the colostomy would not be reversible.

Israel told the doctor that he would not allow the surgery. He said that he would rather die than live his life with a colostomy bag. I really understood how he felt, and I did not try to persuade him to change his mind, but I prayed as hard as I have ever prayed in my life that God would cause Israel's intestine to begin functioning and return him to perfect health. I prayed constantly, and I knew that Israel was going to be healed. Hundreds of people were praying for him, but I told him that it was not enough for other people to pray. Even though he was so sick, he needed to pray too. Every time I gave him that speech he answered, "I know, Mom. I am praying."

The doctor informed Israel that his intestine was not going to begin functioning, but that if he chose to lie in the hospital bed and die, that was his decision. Israel lay there day after day, violently ill and in horrible pain, but after a week with no sign of improvement, his intestine began to come to life once again. Within a few days it was functioning normally! After Israel was released from the hospital, it took him several months to fully recover, but he is once again perfectly healthy and strong.

This attack caused Israel to re-evaluate his goals and focus on his future. He decided that he wants to be a veterinarian. Because he has a liberal arts degree, he needed to take some of the more advanced science courses to be eligible for veterinary school, and he immediately enrolled in required courses in Los Angeles and began earning those credits. Right now he is actively applying at veterinary schools for the 2012 school year.

Gabrielle

When Gabrielle was six years old, she informed me that she wanted to run in a one hundred mile race that she had seen on television. I pointed out that she was too young to enter, but that if she wanted to do so when she was grown, she should consider that all of her competitors would be men. "That's alright," she said, "I can beat them because they'll stop for water, but I'll just keep running."

As she grew older Gabrielle's determination remained intact. She has always wanted to do her own thing in her own way, and she has never welcomed advice. In the fall of 2004 she moved to Seattle, Washington where she went to work as the Operations Manager for a major bank. She stayed there until the spring of 2009 when, after much urging from her family, she returned to El Paso.

She is now employed with a major insurance company and seems to be enjoying her life. Yet, I still see glimpses of that little girl whose strategy for winning the race was to keep running while everyone else stopped for water. Gabrielle remains determined to carve out her own path.

Stefan

Stefan began working for our mortgage company on April 1, 1998—the day that Alexandra opened it. He was sixteen years old at the time and finishing his master's degree. He worked only part time because he was putting the finishing touches on his master's thesis, but from day one he loved Frontier 2000 Mortgage.

During the twelve years that we have been in business Stefan has never wavered in his loyalty and willingness to do everything possible to help the business succeed. He began as Alexandra's loan processor, and when he was older he moved up to become a licensed loan officer. On several occasions he lobbied with us in Washington D.C. and attended numerous conventions in various Texas cities where we took seminars to learn as much as possible about the new mortgage products that became available every year. He is now one of the owners of Frontier 2000 Mortgage.

Nevertheless, Stefan's real strength does not lie in mortgage origination. He is a tremendously gifted writer, and in his spare time writes screen plays. One of them is a comedy that deals with two brothers who love playing flag football more than anything; the problem is that they are just not very good at it. It is a really funny comedy, and when I read the script, I laughed myself silly. Of course, since he had based the script on himself and his brother Judah, I had quite a bit of insight into the craziness of the two boys in the story.

I was, however, not the only one to find the screen play engaging. Stefan entered it in a global screen play contest in which there were fifty thousand entries. He finished in the top one hundred—quite an accomplishment for a first effort.

Stefan is still with us and is still writing. He is currently working on a Christian novel that he hopes to finish within the next year.

Judah

Judah never wanted to be a part of Frontier 2000 Mortgage. When he was sixteen, he went to work for the Brylane call center in El Paso. Soon he was promoted to a supervisory position, and when he was seventeen, he was named Employee of the Year for the call centers. One of the executives flew to El Paso from corporate headquarters in order to personally present his citation at a banquet given in honor of the occasion. Since Judah was still a year away from getting his driver's license, his boss was instructed to drive him to the banquet.

In 2006 Judah made a brief foray into the company business. He came to work at Frontier 2000 and proved to have a real aptitude for the mortgage business. Unlike his sister, however, Judah soon discovered that he was not a small business person.

Judah likes corporate life, and in 2008 he returned to it. He is now a supervisor for United Blood Services. He loves his job and is very happy working for other people.

A Work in Progress

I mentioned that when I began homeschooling I had to get up at five-thirty every morning. That was very hard for me, and I looked forward to the day when I would no longer have to jump out of bed at that hour. That day finally came. My last student received his Master's Degree in 2000, and I began working full-time at Frontier 2000 Mortgage. I no longer get up at five-thirty; I now get up at five o'clock.

I put on my make-up, style my hair, and begin doing housework—I am still on a schedule so that every morning I know exactly what housework needs to be done on that particular day of the week before I leave for work. We have breakfast, Bible reading and prayer before I drive the nine miles to the offices of Frontier 2000 Mortgage where I arrive by nine o'clock. I seldom leave the offices during the day. Normally, I go home between five-thirty and six o'clock. By the time dinner is cooked and the kitchen is cleaned, I may have an hour for television before I go to bed—somewhere between nine-thirty and ten o'clock.

I am so thankful that God has given us a business where I can work with my husband and Alexandra and Stefan. Spending my days with the people I love is a tremendous blessing. I have never been happier, but I know that life is made up of a series of changing circumstances. I try to always be ready for "the next thing."

Although I have been a licensed mortgage loan officer since 2000, when Alexandra became so busy that she needed an assistant, I took on that job. I also do all of the bookkeeping, the payroll and the quarterly taxes—we have an excellent CPA who prepares our year-end taxes. I have enjoyed the challenges of learning a difficult and highly competitive business, and I have loved having the opportunity to help people realize the American Dream of homeownership. We have built our business through word-of-mouth; our client base is comprised primarily of people who have been recommended to us by friends or family members. Who knew that you can still become successful by treating people with respect and dealing with them honestly?

This year as the mortgage industry is in the process of shutting down, Alexandra and I have published *The Fourth Kingdom* and *The Twelfth Juror*, two Christian novels that we co-wrote more than twenty years ago. We also republished *No Regrets: How Homeschooling Earned me a Master's Degree at*

Age Sixteen, which was originally published in 1989. We had wanted very much to publish the novels at the time we wrote them, but it just never worked out for us to do so. This year everything fell into place. Stefan designed the covers for both novels. For the cover of *The Twelfth Juror,* Israel allowed us to use his drawing of the face of the beautiful blonde woman with the emerald eyes. Seeing those novels become a reality was a dream come true for both Alexandra and me.

In reflecting on the years I spent homeschooling my children, I like to think that if I could go back and do it all over again, I would do a better job this time. The regrets that I have stem from my own small acts of unkindness towards my children. I wish that I had been more patient and more understanding with them. I sometimes imagine that in the saga of *The Swann Homeschool* "take two" I would be the perfect Mother.

Going back is, of course, not an option, and it is also not a guarantee that if I could, I would actually do a better job this time. First of all, I would not have the luxury of hindsight and would probably repeat many of the same mistakes. Even if I did have the advantage of hindsight and I chose to do everything differently, that is not a guarantee that I would do a better job—I might not do as well.

I also remind myself that I homeschooled based on who I am. Every educator brings a great deal of herself into the classroom. How she deals with her students, the approaches she takes to both teaching and learning, and the way she structures her classroom are all reflections of her own world view.

When the children were taking sociology classes at BYU, we read about a study of twins that included the "Jim twins." They were identical twin boys adopted at birth by different families who named both boys Jim. Although they had grown up within a few miles of each other, neither was aware of the other's existence. When the Jims were in their mid-forties, they were reunited, and the similarities between their lives was startling. Each had been married twice. Both first wives bore the same name, and each of their second wives also bore the same name. Each had two children—a boy and a girl—and the children had the same names. They owned same breed of dog—with the same name. They wore their hair the same way, and they were employed in the same profession. The list of similarities went on and on.

The sociology text said that identical twins who are raised together are less alike than those who are raised separately. The reasoning is that twins who are raised together make an effort to be less like their twins while those who are unaware of the other's existence do not resist becoming the people they really are. Consequently, those twins tend to be very much alike.

Perhaps, if I could go back without hindsight, "take two" would be "the Joyce twin." At any rate, I can be absolutely certain that under no circumstances would I have been the perfect mother.

Would I do it again? Absolutely! I consider it a great privilege to have been given the opportunity to teach my children at home. Every hour spent with them was a gift from God. I have a myriad of precious memories that would never have been mine if I had put them on a big yellow bus every morning and waived good-by as they rode off to spend their days among strangers.

We shared more as a family than we would have been able to under any other circumstances. Some memories cause tears to well up in my eyes as I recall illnesses and hardships that I wish I could have prevented them from having to endure. Others make me smile when I remember the funny things they did or said. But every memory, whether it evokes laughter or tears, is a precious jewel that continues to enrich my life.

I have tried to run a good race. I have homeschooled to the best of my ability. I have been the best loan originator and assistant that I knew how to be. The novels that Alexandra and I wrote together are a true labor of love that I pray will bless all who read them and touch them in ways that will help them experience the love and Grace that can only be found in Jesus Christ. I am painfully aware that I have fallen short in every area, but I am still a work in progress, and I hope above everything else that God will use me to further His kingdom here on earth.

On September 11, 2010, I watched part of a televised memorial service at Ground Zero. One of the families who had lost a loved one in the attacks was represented by a grandmother who had lost her son-in-law in the towers. She read a heart-rending message to him about how much he was missed and how much she wished that he could see the fine young women that his two daughters had become.

She closed with these words, "If love could have saved you, you would all have lived forever."

Those words haunt me because they remind me once again that the world is filled with people who do not know about the only love strong enough to save us so that we can live forever. It is my hope that through our books Alexandra and I will be able to reach many people like that woman and tell them the good news: Jesus lives, and because of His love, all who receive Him will live forever.

ABOUT THE AUTHOR

Joyce Swann homeschooled her ten children from the first grade through master's degrees. She is a well-known author and speaker on the subject of homeschooling. For many years she was a popular columnist for *Practical Homeschooling Magazine*. She now blogs regularly on parenting and homeschooling issues.

Joyce has co-authored two novels, *The Fourth Kingdom* and *The Twelfth Juror,* both of which were published in 2010. Her children's stories *Tales of Pig Isle,* also published in 2010, began as stories that Joyce told to entertain her grandchildren.

Looking Backward: My Twenty-Five Years as a Homeschooling Mother chronicles her personal story of her experiences raising and educating her family. Today, Joyce and her husband, John, live in Anthony, New Mexico, in the same house where they raised their family.